Using the Bible in Drama

Steve and Janet Stickley and Jim Belben

Series Editor:
Wendy S. Robins

Bible Society

© BFBS 1980   7m
second impression 1981

This publication by the Bible Society,
146 Queen Victoria Street, London EC4V 4BX

ISBN 0 564 00990 3

Contents

1 - 75

The Authors

Steve and Janet Stickley met whilst at college and were married in 1975. Specializing in drama they formed the Footprints Theatre Company on New Year's Eve 1978 and have toured the country with it ever since. Major events include the Scripture Union Centenary Road Show — "One in the Eye", Greenbelt, "Up the Wall," and a tour of Scotland and the Shetland Isles.

Jim Belben has been Youth Officer with Bible Society since 1978. Before that he studied at Keele and Sussex Universities. He writes material for Christian drama groups, but his own acting career has been cut short by a tendency to sneeze at moments of tension!

Steve and Janet would like to express their thanks to the following Footprints (past and present) for all their talents used in the creation of the published scripts:
Phil
Nigel and Lizzie
Alan
Mark
Chris
and Lance.

Introduction

I have memories of three particular Sunday services when I was at school. The first is when the boy in the seat two along from me was sick during the prayers. The sound is what I remember — like a half-pound bag of peanuts spilling onto the floor. The second is when a large glass-fronted print of Constable's "Haywain", at least three feet by two feet, crashed to the floor in the middle of the sermon. The glass smashed into ten thousand pieces. The preacher stopped, stared, waited and then carried on, or attempted to, as though nothing had happened. The third is of a different church in which the pulpit was raised twelve feet above floor level. The preacher in his agitated delivery jumped around the pulpit. At one point he swung his arms so violently that he dislodged a pile of academic-looking volumes which he had presumably intended to refer to in his fifty minute sermon, but which now lay scattered around the front of the church.

If we had had drama in our services, I might have remembered more. But long after all the sermons I heard have melted away, the disasters and accidents remain in my mind, because they are interesting. They were *sounds*, *pictures*, and *entertainment*! Drama serves the same purpose. It offers sounds and pictures and entertainment, instead of endless dry monologues, which is why the Bible Society is so keen that it should be used in presenting the Bible.

There is more to it however. Just being involved in drama can deepen a person's experience of the Bible, and Christian fellowship. In fact my own experience of drama has been that it breaks down barriers, it livens up a group's life, it uses people's hidden skills, it helps people trust one another, it brings a new dimension to the Bible, it entertains, teaches, and much more.

This book is largely the work of Steve and Janet Stickley. They have spent the last four years — two years as leaders of Footprints Theatre Co. — in leading workshops and performing around Great Britain. Their experience has made this as practical a resource book for Christian drama as you will find.

Try it and see.

Jim Belben
Youth Officer
Bible Society

6

1 Starting a Drama Group

1. You can do it too

The villain in a ginger-coloured wig, with a red nose and a long flowing black cape, has finished talking with the pin-stripe suited banker who is sitting by the lectern. Now, with an hysterical horror-movie laugh he prances across the front of your church ready to throttle the little old-age pensioner huddled in her wheel-chair underneath the pulpit. The pensioner has not paid her rent, so she's going to suffer. The villain has not paid his overdraft but the banker has let him off it.

Surely the banker will not allow this now he has seen how little mercy the villain has on the old lady!

Your congregation is angry. Most of them know this story from Matthew 18, but they are seeing it again with a new poignancy. Not only the kids, but everybody at this family service will remember the injustice of the villain, the mercy and judgement of the banker, the defencelessness of the pensioner.

In the audience the minister, a church warden, a youth leader, and a church member are all thinking "Surely we can do this more often!" and "Why don't we set up a drama group?"

Why not?

Of course you can still have drama in church without a drama group, but a consistent group can be so much more ambitious and reliable than a group convened specially to do an occasional sketch. So if you think there might be room for a drama group in your church or organization, read on.

What you need

A leader

This book is written for the leader. The leader should have time to commit to the group — about three hours a week at least; should have some experience in leading groups; should be in sympathy with the aims of the church; and should be a creative person with an ability to inspire others. If that sounds like a job description for Superman, then concentrate on the first bit. A leader without a deep commitment to the group will be a failure. If you do not feel that you are this person, pass the book on to someone whom you think might be suitable.

A group

You don't need all the group to be keen actors or extroverts though you will need one or two! Anyone can learn from drama and get involved in it even if they are not naturally cut out to be performers. Once again commitment is the most important quality — not long-term commitment, but an all-out commitment to the group in all its activities for as long as they are members. To be realistic, you may be well advised to think in terms of a trial run, and we suggest your group has an initial life of six months, after which people can back out with diginity if it seems too much.

A church

The group's main loyalty should be to the church (or other organization) to which its members belong. Acceptance will only come in return for a loyal contribution to the life of the church. Even if a group is intending to concentrate on work outside the church, the church is still its reference point. In the past, some drama groups have felt alienated because the church does not seem to accept the group's "ministry". All too often this has been because the group did not see *itself* as part of the church. It's worth getting this right at the start.

A minister

One way to do this is to draw the minister or leader in as a consultant. When the drama group's task is to understand, interpret, and present the Bible, the skills of the minister will be indispensible. The group could consider him to be their "theological consultant", if they want to make the relationship sound official. You may sometimes find yourselves also in need of advice and pastoral assistance which the minister is probably the best person to offer.

Opportunities

There is a lot more about this later, but it is important to say at this stage that a drama group is there to be used. Whenever an opportunity exists for the growing skills of the group to be used in worship, evangelism, entertainment or encouragement, then use them. It will help the group to grow in confidence and maturity, and will give the church a window into the life of the group.

Using this book

This is a resource book. We don't intend you to pick it up and read it straight through like a novel.

Chapter 1 deals with the basic questions that any group will have to answer, such as: What should be the size of our group? What will we do when we meet together?

Chapter 2 gives a large range of ideas that you can use in designing sessions for your group.

Chapter 3 gives guidance on how to present and perform your drama when you are ready.

Chapter 4 gives some sample scripts by Footprints Theatre Co.

Because it is a resource book, some of it might not be relevant to you at first. But however limited your ambitions are — even if you only want to put on a three-minute sketch in church — you will still benefit by being familiar with basic tools such as drama, games and improvisation. So get to know Chapter 1 to start with, and discover the importance of the basic tools. But, first things first!

Getting your group together

Aims
It's important to know *why* you want to have a group. It will probably be for one or a mixture of the following reasons:
○ to perform sketches in Sunday worship or other church activity
○ to use drama in outreach or entertainment in your local community
○ to grow together as a group
If you know what your aims are, it will help you to select members, as you will need people who are enthusiastic about those aims.

Size
Five to eight people is an ideal number. Larger and the group becomes less sensitive to each other. Smaller and you may not have enough people for the drama you want to do. If you by any chance have too many people who are interested, then it is important to identify those who are most suitable. The most diplomatic way to do this is to let them select themselves — begin with one or two imaginatively demanding sessions, and explain how much time and commitment is expected. This should deter the faint-hearted.

Supporters
Do beware of people who say they would like to be involved "from time to time" or "when you've got something special on", as a half-hearted commitment can be worse than none at all. If there are people who want to be involved but genuinely do not have the time to commit themselves to regular meetings, then there are jobs which they can do to contribute to the success of the group e.g. publicity; making and maintaining costumes and props; arranging transport for the group if you are performing away from home; keeping an account of group expenses; contacting and liaising with churches or other people who

invite you to visit them. On the other hand you can encourage a sense of shared responsibility in the group if these jobs are taken on by group members.

Variety
Fling the net wide when you recruit. Do not limit yourself to one particular sub-group of the church. Invite unexpected people to join the group. Any barriers between its members will be broken down by the activities in which they take part, *as long as they are committed* from the start to the aims of the group.

Leadership
Obviously, a lot will depend on you as leader of the group. You are mainly responsible for keeping the group on course — to do what it set out to do — and although drama is a group experience, as in most group work, things will soon go awry without clear leadership. But you are not a dictator, taking all responsibilities and making all decisions. You must be ready to accept suggestions and ideas from the others, and to offer them responsibility as often as possible. You must join in with activities as one of the group. If you have only a little experience you may be tempted to lord it over the others and hide your insecurity by pretending to know more than you do. It is much better to be honest about your inexperience and to set off to learn together as a group.

Planning your programme

2. Designing group sessions
Weekly
It is best for a group to have a regular weekly meeting, preferably about two hours long. This could be one evening, but it is even better on a Saturday during the day-time (when people are less likely to be tired from a hard day at school, college or work).

Large space
A fairly large space with plenty of room for moving around is needed — rather conveniently this makes church halls an ideal setting, but do make sure there is nothing going on nearby, as you need to be able to let your hair down without fear of disturbing anyone. Try to plan it so that you won't be disturbed either. It is very frustrating to get involved in a scene and then to have to move so that someone can set out chairs for a meeting!

Privacy
People may sometimes ask you if they can come in and "watch" one of your sessions. It is best to say "no", as the feeling of being watched

often makes it difficult to concentrate and all sorts of inhibitions may appear. On the other hand, in the later stages of rehearsing for a performance a few selected observers can be quite helpful as a test audience to watch you perform, and afterwards offer you their frank comments.

Types of session

Always have something purposeful planned for your sessions, otherwise you will quickly become bored and demoralized. You should plan too much for each session and drop some of it, rather than planning too little and then having to pad it out. Ensure a variety of sessions rather than doing the same thing every week. Although this will require a lot of imagination and energy to start with, as you progress you will find it increasingly easy to design sessions for your group, and other members will be able to take responsibility. There cannot be one blueprint for all sessions, as both the type of session and its content will depend on what you want to achieve in it. Look at Diagram 1, which introduces the types of sessions which you will want to have, and what they should contain.

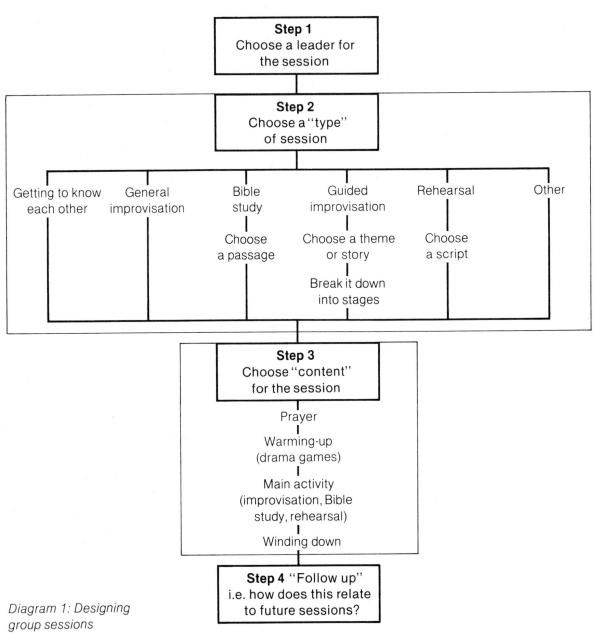

Step 1
Choose a leader for the session

Step 2
Choose a "type" of session

Getting to know each other

General improvisation

Bible study

Choose a passage

Guided improvisation

Choose a theme or story

Break it down into stages

Rehearsal

Choose a script

Other

Step 3
Choose "content" for the session

Prayer

Warming-up (drama games)

Main activity (improvisation, Bible study, rehearsal)

Winding down

Step 4 "Follow up" i.e. how does this relate to future sessions?

Diagram 1: Designing group sessions

Sample programme

Try to balance your group's programme between sessions of all kinds. We cannot be sure what is appropriate for your group because it must be tailored to your particular needs, but a sample schedule for the first twelve weeks of a group's life could look like this. Sample sessions 1-4 are included in this book, and they could if you wished form the first four sessions of your group.

1. Getting to know each other session (page 27). Various light-hearted drama games and improvisation exercises.

2. General improvisation (page 32). Discovering various improvisation exercises, but in an open-ended session.

3. Bible study on the Sower (page 39). Discovering how to understand the Sower and how to break down the passage into themes/scenes.

4. Guided improvisation 1 (page 33). Discovering how treating one theme from a number of angles can produce enough material to create a sketch.

5. Guided improvisation 2. Continuing the process of creating a sketch out of the improvised material of last week.

6. Choice between going out to the theatre together, or rehearsing someone else's material, e.g. "The Race" (page 93).

7. Bible study on the parable of the Sheep and Goats.

8. Guided improvisation on the theme of how people respond to others' suffering.

9. The previous sessions having revealed that one of the group's weak points is, for example, lack of free and adventurous physical movement, you could now have a session devoted to that point, i.e. games and improvisations which encourage free movement, and mime skills.

10. Bible study on the story of Gideon.

11. Rehearsing two sketches from those that you have evolved or rehearsed.

12. Performing.

Your sessions will be built from a variety of the following:

Drama games

The importance of these games is that they loosen up the group, relax inhibitions, and develop certain essential dramatic skills. Remember:

○ *You are never too good* to miss out these games and go straight into the next stages. Even the most professional companies continue to develop their abilities by doing drama games such as those in Chapter 2 and by inventing new ones.

○ *Do not try to do too much.* Two games well done and used to maximum effect will be quite enough for one session. You should not spend much more than 20 minutes of a two hour session on these games.

○ *Use the same game in a number of sessions.* They will bear repeating until you are familiar with them. If they do get at all stale, most of them can be varied slightly to prevent over-familiarity. It could take you up to fifty sessions to use all the games listed in Chapter 2!

○ The biggest difficulty your group will have to face is inhibition and embarrassment. In choosing games, therefore, remember that they are designed to *help the group relax* and get to know one another.

○ Always attempt to *make the games fit what is to follow* in the session, e.g. if you want to do a session on "dreams" you could begin with the waking up game on page 21. In the same way use games sensibly, to develop certain skills which your group is weak in, e.g. voice production (page 24).

Drama games are dealt with in detail in Chapter 2.

Improvisation

Improvisation has many purposes. Most important, through experimenting with a wide variety of characters and situations it helps your group to discover their potential as actors, and it gets over the problem of how to create scripts and sketches if you are no good at writing! People use the phrase "I had to improvise" as a way of saying "I had to make do with what I had available". In music, improvisation describes a rambling style of jazz or rock. In drama it can mean much more than this. Improvisation is an exciting and ideal way of exploring and experiencing feelings or stories, and creating drama.

Improvisation is discussed in detail in Chapter 2. Improvisation sessions will be of two types:

○ General improvisation, which is really just a "fun" session in which you experiment with a number of different situations and characters. General improvisation exercises from Chapter 2 can be included in any session.

○ Guided improvisation, where the leader prepares a series of improvisation exercises around a certain theme, leading to a specific end. You will never use more than half a dozen of the improvisation exercises in any one session, whatever type of session you are doing. Improvisation must be given time to grow and mature, not be rushed.

Devote a whole session every two or three weeks to improvisation, either general or guided. General improvisation needs as much leadership as guided improvisation, but in the former the leader can afford to experiment with a wide variety of exercises. Note also that the leader should not just design the session, but should lead it (making clear to the group at all stages what they should be doing and why), and should also be sure how this session fits into the overall programme for the group, i.e. Does it lead to a performance? Is it just for fun? Is it to interpret a Bible passage that particularly interests the group?

Bible study

Most of this book is about drama in general, and not about the Bible. The reason is that we believe that the Bible will be used best if the group have a grasp of the basic drama tools. No one would dream of sending a musician on stage without first teaching him how to play or sing. Neither should we assume that we can put actors out in front of an audience without being taught about drama. All too often we think that acting comes naturally, whereas in fact it takes a good deal of application and hard work.

The Bible is *the best resource book* for a Christian drama group. The Bible is full of stories and events that are appropriate for drama. What's more, when a lot of contemporary drama concerns itself with very superficial matters, the Bible is a stock of material worth communicating, which strikes deep into people's lives. Most important, however, the Bible needs translating again. It needs translating out of "The Big Black Book" into other media, and you can be part of the translation team when turning it into drama.

As a group, this gives you certain responsibilities: both to understand what the Bible is saying, and to find and understand the audience who

need to hear this message. When you come to the section on Bible study in Chapter 2, you will discover that these two responsibilities go hand in hand.

Not all your drama will be stories from the Bible. Modern life is full of stories that will be worth your while studying and working on. The Bible should be your unifying theme, however, and be so central to the life of your group that your drama, even when it does not directly present the Bible, grows out of it. We suggest that you study the Bible together at least once every three sessions. A Bible study session can be built into another session, or it can be a separate session all on its own.

Rehearsal and performance

Successful performances are a real boost to a group's confidence but when they are unsuccessful they are just the opposite, so don't perform until you are ready for it! Drama for its own sake, as an exciting group experience, could be much more relevant than performance in this case. In the normal run of your group's life, however, you should try to get an opportunity to perform within the first three months, as this will help the group take the sessions seriously. This will mean that some of your weekly sessions will be taken up with rehearsing the material that you are going to present, and it might also entail fixing a couple of extra rehearsal sessions near to the time of the performance.

Other activities

Drama involves people on almost every level — mental, physical, emotional, spiritual and social. It involves experiencing new feelings and emotions and helping others to experience them as well. This will usually mean that the group will find it easier to pray together, share problems and be open with each other. Encourage this by meeting together for fellowship, and for social trips, e.g. to the cinema or theatre. This will also give you the chance to pick up tips from the professionals.

Leading sessions

It is important that the pace of sessions should not be allowed to flag, and that the concentration of the group should be maintained. This is a lot easier when you are doing group work than when you are rehearsing. If sessions regularly break up into disarray and people seem unable to take them seriously, then you should plan for more physically strenuous activity, and more exercises that aid concentration. As far as possible all the group should be involved in the activities at the same time.

On the other hand, do not be afraid of pauses, and moments of relaxation. You do not have to keep up a frantic pace throughout your two hour session. Particularly when the group splits up into smaller groups to work together, do not be tied by your own timetable as to how long to give them, but notice when they are ready to be called back together again. In your own preparation, however, it is important to include for yourself an approximate estimate of how long an activity will take.

You must have sensitivity to the mood of the group, listening to what they want to do and not always ploughing on with your own plans. As we said before, you are not a dictator, but an enabler — you enable the group to do drama — which might sometimes mean chairing heated discussions, praying for patience, or fighting against the waves of apathy which will wash over the group from time to time. In fact, the very idea of a structure to a drama group's activity is difficult to maintain, because output often consists of one part structure and ninety-nine parts inspiration!

Start sessions with prayer. This will help the group to realize that what it does is being done for God. You might also consider beginning sessions with a provocative meditation which sets the group thinking about issues relevant to the session. A picture passed round the group, to which everybody puts a caption; a poem; a piece of music; a newspaper story: these can all help create an atmosphere which helps the group to work. On the same note, try not to end sessions abruptly. Instead try and wind people down:
○ either by inviting feedback and discussion on what has been done in the session;
○ or by encouraging thought about the session — through prayer, music, or silence.
A good session will stay in the group's mind in the week that follows, and this should be encouraged. You will quickly learn what your group responds to and what it dislikes.

As for sharing leadership, encourage others to take responsibility for the occasional session. If the group do not respond well to a particular person's leadership, however, limit that person's role to a supporting one — leading one exercise for instance. The group must have confidence in the session leader.

2

Resources

1. Drama games

To help you choose the right games for your group we have put the games under headings which show which skill they mainly encourage, although these categories are by no means exclusive and are bound to overlap with each other.

Warming up

The good actor is always aware of his body, and has control over it as he uses it to communicate to his audience. To have control over your body you need to be physically fit and muscles which may have been asleep for years need rediscovering, waking up and keeping in full working order. Any keep fit exercise which stretches you and your muscles will be suitable, but it is best to start off with something comparatively gentle otherwise you might end up with a pulled muscle! Ideas for warm-up games:

Old King Cole

Stand in a small circle with shoulders almost touching, hands by your sides, feet together. As a group recite the first two lines of the nursery rhyme Old King Cole, treating the bold phrases as one word:

"Old King Cole **was a** merry old soul,

And a merry old soul **was a** he!"

Now repeat the rhyme saying one word each, going round the circle in a clockwise direction.

i.e. Person A "Old"

Person B "King"

Person C "Cole"

Person D "was a" etc.

Repeat this, going round the circle several times until a good rhythm has built up, and so that there are no perceivable "gaps". Now comes the difficult bit! When a person says "was a", he or she bobs down and then quickly up again in time to the rhythm. When someone says "and a", everyone bobs down and up silently. Try this out and you will soon discover the physical co-ordination required — it is not as easy as it sounds! Old King Cole can be played as a knock-out game i.e. when somebody makes a mistake they are awarded a "black mark". Three "black marks" and they are out. Aim to get proficient at this until you can recite the rhyme and bob up and down faultlessly in five seconds.

Do you see what this game demands? Each person must be aware of the whole game all the time. Concentration and physical co-ordination are essential, and a good sense of rhythm is developed and shared by

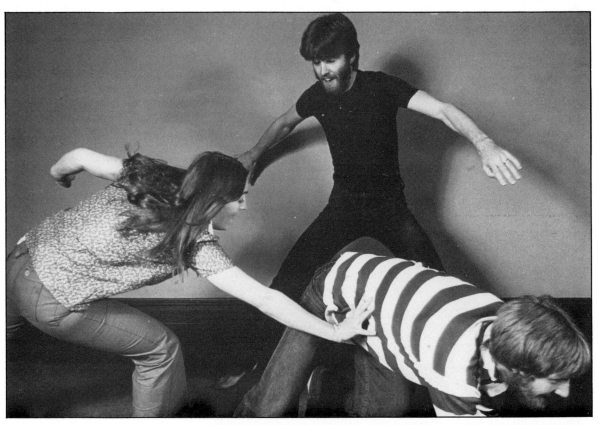

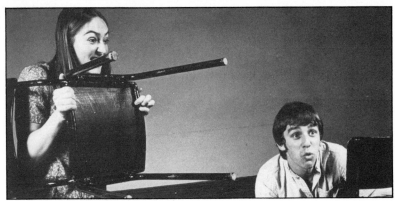

the group who are working together to achieve a final effect similar to that of a fast-moving rhythmic style of narration, which could form the backbone of a slick and powerful sketch.

Waking-up

All the group lie out flat on their backs and relax for two minutes completely, as if they were asleep. The leader now encourages each person to concentrate on each part of their body independently, discovering and stretching it and flexing its muscles. Begin with a foot, then move up the body — calf, knee etc. until you come to the head. Once all the body has been discovered, people can then stand up and the leader can lead them into other exercises.

Keep-fit exercises

One way of using keep-fit exercises is for all the group to face in the same direction towards a leader. They have to copy whatever the leader does be it star-jumps, press-ups, somersaults or whatever.

Childhood games

Childhood games are an inexhaustible supply of physically demanding yet simple games which also relax the group. Rediscover them for yourselves: "What's the time, Mr. Wolf?", "Grandmother's footsteps", "Stick in the Mud", "Off ground tig", "Chain he", and any versions of tig or hide and seek can be used.

Imagination

Objects

Take a familiar object, a chair for example, and compete to see who can *use it in the most inventive ways*. It may become an anti-aircraft gun, a train, a space capsule, a pram, a great work of art etc. Try it so that everyone has the same object to work with, and on a given signal (a bang on a drum for instance) they have to change the use they put it to. A development of this is to work in pairs with one object between you.

Word association

The group sit in a circle and one person starts the game by saying a word, the person next to them has to follow it with another word which either rhymes or is directly linked with it, and so on. A good speed should be built up, and no repetition is allowed! If this gets too easy, try playing it to a strict rhythm of three beats, e.g. for the first two beats everyone pats their knees, on the third beat they click their fingers and the next person says their word. Yet another variation is word disassociation — a surprisingly difficult version where each word must have *nothing at all* to do with the previous one!

Sounds

Record various everyday sounds.on a cassette tape and see how many the group can identify. This can be developed into small groups of people making recordings using the stories of familiar nursery rhymes or fairy stories, such as Little Red Riding Hood, without using words — just sound effects. See if the others in the group can recognize the story.

Memory

Armadillo

1. "I went to market and I bought an Armadillo . . ."
2. "I went to market and I bought an Armadillo and a Brush . . ."
3. "I went to market and I bought an Armadillo, a Brush and a Crow . . ."

As this game progresses through the alphabet, each person must *repeat the whole list* adding an article of their own choosing. A variation can be to have all the articles beginning with a common letter.

Kim's game

Put about twenty different objects on a tray and cover them with a cloth. Take the cloth away for sixty seconds and let the group study the objects, then cover them up again. Get everyone to write down as many objects as they can recall with a little detail e.g. a red, plastic thimble; a square, silver brooch etc. This can be repeated with different objects and a progressively shorter amount of time for studying them.

Obstacles

Arrange various large obstacles around the room and let a person walk around the course for sixty seconds. Stand them at a particular starting point and then blindfold them. They have to walk around the course or climb over the objects remembering the shape, size and position of the various obstacles. Vary the course for each person, perhaps decreasing the amount of time they have to study it before putting on the blindfold.

Mime skills

Charades

Take it in turn to mime the title of a film, book or television programme for the rest of the group to guess. Concentrate on making your mime as definite and simple as possible. A more exciting and competitive variation involves forming two teams with one person from each team deciding together on a subject to mime. Each returns to their respective team and attempts to communicate the chosen subject in the simplest most effective mime possible. (Mouthing words is strictly forbidden!) The first team to guess the subject is awarded a point.

Shaving

Everyone sits in a circle, one person gets up and goes into the middle of the circle and begins miming an activity, e.g. shaving. The next person in the circle asks him "What are you doing?" and whilst continuing shaving he replies with an idea for a new activity, such as milking a cow. The first person then sits down again in his place in the circle and is replaced by the second who mimes milking a cow. This continues as the third person asks "What are you doing"? and the second replies, for example, "Mowing the lawn". Person three then replaces him and mimes mowing a lawn and so on. The aim is for the game to move quickly and at a smooth rate without mistakes.

Photographs

Split into two teams and prepare a tableau (a scene in which all the characters are "frozen") which depicts a famous event or historic moment, e.g. the stabbing of Julius Caesar, or Sir Walter Raleigh putting his cloak over the puddle for Queen Elizabeth. See if the other team can guess the event just from the "photograph" before them. To introduce more discipline, it is a good idea to put a time limit on the preparation of the tableau.

Voice control and production

Tongue-twisters

Get hold of a *book of tongue-twisters* and practise saying them quickly and clearly. Compete to see who can say them the highest number of times, most coherently, within a given time limit. Write your own tongue-twisters. Set well-known tongue-twisters to music and sing them together. Try singing "Pa's got a head like a ping-pong ball" to the tune of William Tell's Overture, playing about with the "pings" and "pongs" to make the words fit the tune. When you've mastered this try changing the first letter, e.g. "Ma's got a med like a ming mong mawl" and so on, making the mouth really work at making different shapes. (One of the most difficult prefixes is "Sq".)

Dictation

Split the group into pairs. Call one person "A", the other "B". Sit all the "A"s at one end of the room with a pen and paper. Put the "B"s at the other end of the room opposite their partners and issue each one with a different piece of written material, e.g. an extract from a story, a recipe, a knitting pattern, a newspaper article etc. On a given signal, the "B"s must start dictating their pieces to their partners who must write them down. The dictation should include all punctuation etc. As they are all speaking at once the "B"s have to take considerable care to make their speech clear and loud. The winning pair are the ones who, at a given stop signal, have written the most words and made the least mistakes. N.B. This only works if you have at least six people.

Soapboxes

Two people stand facing each other on chairs about one foot apart. Each is given a different subject to speak on, e.g. knitting bed socks, stuffing a cat, my granny's knees etc. On a given signal they both begin to speak whilst looking each other directly in the eye. The one who succeeds in making his partner laugh or "dry up" is the winner.

Letters and papers

Each member brings a letter they have received, or is given a page of a newspaper. The leader then instructs them to read it out loud (together, but not in unison) in the manner of a chosen emotion — tearfully, boringly, lethargically, laughingly, angrily, happily etc. etc. A second stage to this game, once people are loosened up, is for just one person to read their passage, e.g. tearfully, and for others to *respond* in an appropriate fashion.

Trust

Another method of encouraging relationships within the group is by the use of simple trust exercises.

Stiff

Get into groups of three, labelling yourselves A, B and C. A and C stand facing each other about three feet apart. Person B stands mid-way between them, facing A:

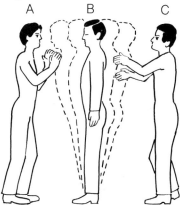

Person B closes his eyes and putting his hands by his sides imagines that he is stiff and rigid like a block of wood. Very gently A pushes B off balance towards C, who catches him as he rocks backwards on his heels still remaining stiff as a board. C pushes him back towards A who catches him and returns him again. This continues as A and C gradually move further apart, allowing B to tip backwards and forwards at a greater angle before they catch him. If B feels that he cannot trust A and C, he will not be able to remain rigid and the exercise will fail. The whole exercise should be carried out in silence with A and C each concentrating on safely catching and gently pushing B. Change over roles until everyone has had a go at "trusting" their friends. If you have a large enough group who are sensible enough not to betray each other's trust, then this can progress to exercises where someone falls backwards off a chair, then a table and perhaps even a piano and is caught by the rest of the group who stand arms outstretched in a reassuring manner. If undertaken lightly some of these exercises could obviously be very dangerous and if you would be happier with something less hair-raising then try this:

Partners

Put blindfolds on several people and secretly select partners for them who will lead them outside on a short journey. Again this should be done in silence, each "blind" person encountering obstacles with the unspoken help of their sighted partners. Aim to build up a relationship of

trust between the two partners so that they will be able to do quite daring operations together — such as running! It is more difficult than it sounds. Once back inside again remove the blindfolds and see if each "blind" person can identify his or her partner. Notice how it felt to have put all your trust in someone else, and also how it felt to have someone trust you completely, or not to trust you at all, as the case may be!

Shapes

With eyes closed, one group member has to go round the rest of the group who are sitting in a circle, guessing who they are, just by feeling their hands and faces. Once they have done this, another group member takes his turn, but first all the group change places in the circle. This game obviously has more relevance in the early unfamiliar stages of a group's life than later, when they know each other better.

Keep a *notebook* of your own where you can jot down ideas for games, and encourage everyone to delve into their own past and remember games they played as children which could prove useful. If there are seven of you in your group and each remembers three games, you have twenty-one to start with! In this way you will soon discover how important your past experience is to your drama. However, if you are still short on ideas, a useful book is Children's Games of Street and Playground by Peter and Iona Opie (see Bibliography).

Sample Session
Getting to know each other

This is session 1 in the sample programme on page 13. It contains some more drama games that are not listed in this chapter, and allows you to experiment in leading a session. Notice particularly how the group responds to the various activities, and what they find easy to do. Timings are approximate.

1. Prayer

Focus on the work you are going to do and ask for God's help.

5 minutes

2. Warming up

Having explained the importance of the body in Drama, get all the group to face in the same direction, towards the leader, and copy his/her actions — which can include any sort of physical jerks, press-ups, star jumps, disco-dancing steps etc. *10 minutes.*

3. Introductions

Invite one group member to state their name, and something about themselves, e.g. "I hate rice pudding" or "I am nervous", and if possible to say it in a voice and with actions that express how they feel. The person to their right then repeats the first person's introduction, as exactly as possible, i.e. mannerisms, voice inflexion etc., and then adds their own introduction. The third person then repeats both introductions and adds their own, until the last person is attempting to repeat the whole group's introductions. This need not be taken seriously, and should provoke a lot of laughter, as well as relaxing the group and familiarizing them with each other.   *20 minutes*

4. Rhythm game

Any game which gets the group working together as a team is useful. It will help the leader to see who in the group is sharp and attentive. This game also helps recall names, if that is a weak point in your group. Sitting in a circle, set up a rhythm of slapping knees twice, clapping twice, and clicking your fingers, each hand separately, right hand first, then left hand, in succession, so that in effect you are counting a six beat rhythm. Once this is established, on the click of your right fingers say your own name, and on the click of your left fingers say the name of someone else in the group who then takes the "lead". Keeping the rhythm going, they then do the same, passing the "lead" on to someone else, by saying their own name and then that other person's name. Anyone who breaks the rhythm has a point against them. After a certain number of points (say 5) they are out.   *10 minutes*

5. Park-bench dialogue

Although this is only a "get-to-know-you" session, it is important that it bears some relation to the kind of activity that you will be doing in later sessions. This is a basic improvisation exercise which develops confidence. Invite the group to split into pairs, sitting next to each other on two chairs, and to invent a park-bench dialogue between two characters, e.g. a mother with her baby and a city gent reading a paper entitled "I think the problem with this country is . . ." Each person in turn moans about Great Britain, and the other person can either respond with disinterest or with argument. Concentrate on developing a voice and a character rather than the reasoned logic of your argument. Give the group 10 minutes to work on their dialogues, then ask each pair to perform them for the rest of the group, discussing them with each other after each dialogue — what was good/funny/sad/unconvincing.
        30 minutes

6. Music and meditation

Don't overload the session, and if you have all had enough to enthuse you, excite you, or kill you off, miss this exercise out. Invite group members to relax, perhaps lying on the floor, and play some "mood-creating" music. With eyes closed, allow their minds to create a picture of what the music conjures up. Discuss the scenes people saw.
        15 minutes

This session will introduce the group to each other, and to the main kinds of group exercises they will be doing in the future. It also introduces you, the leader, to the basic design of a session.

2. Improvisation
Many of the things that drama games have begun will be carried on by improvisation. Improvisation helps to develop your *imagination and confidence*. Improvisation also helps you rediscover all the natural skills you already have, for the purposes of drama – those that you use throughout your life to communicate with others, to explain things, to assert opinions, to make friends, to be sympathetic, to express love or frustration. You have built up a stock of gestures, mannerisms and voice inflexions that you can rediscover for drama.

Improvisation is a means of creating drama without writing. It creates a stock of characters and situations that you can pick up and use in your performances. When a broadcaster makes a T.V. documentary, he will often record more than a hundred hours of films and interviews just to create a one hour film. Likewise, in improvisation you will explore maybe hundreds of characters and situations and discard most of them – but just a few will be useful to create a sketch, or to present the Bible.

Stage 1
Situations

Before you can act out how another character behaves, you have to get to know how you behave. Stage 1 is therefore *being yourself in a given situation*. It is also best if at this early stage people do these exercises on their own, but at the same time as the rest of the group – so they know they are not being watched. Give people a situation that they find themselves in for about four or five minutes, not just miming, but talking to other imaginary characters. Then follow this up with another. Try some of these:

Absurd
    handcuffed to a lamp post
    accidentally smashing a toilet in Buckingham Palace
    finding a hippopotamus in the Post Office etc.
Finding yourself locked out of your car
Carrying a trayful of drinks on a bumpy train
Going quietly up creaky stairs
Lost in London

In a dentist's chair
Robbing a shop
Making a telephone call
Catching a mouse in a bucket
Putting up a deck-chair that won't stay up
Watering the garden with a leaky hose.

There is no limit to your list. This is just to set you on your way.

Stage 2
Characters

You will need to move next into *playing another character in a given situation*. Again as individuals each person takes a character and experiences life as that character. Use one of the situations above, or another of your own choosing, that particularly suits the character, e.g. a wealthy industrialist making a telephone call in the back of his Rolls Royce. Repeat the exercise for a number of characters, giving about five minutes for each character.

Worried mother
Spoilt little girl
Naughty schoolboy
Wealthy industrialist (usually Northern)
Lord or Lady
Scatterbrained old lady
Tramp
Teacher — bossy or sarcastic
Social Worker — well-meaning but weak
Army officer
Filmstar
Door-to-door salesman
Vicar
Fat politician
Punk rocker
Hippie or dropout
Shop steward
Effeminate man
Masculine woman
Nagging wife
Hen-pecked husband
Sadistic dentist

Incompetent doctor
Policeman
A drunk

Another way of creating characters is to provide your group with a box full of hats and coats. Each member takes one and invents a character around it. Or again, send your group out around the town to observe one interesting character, and ask them to show him/her to the group when everybody returns, by acting out his/her habits, actions and mannerisms. Get into the habit of watching people and noticing what is distinctive about them.

Stage 3
Working in pairs

In almost all sessions of improvisation you will want to *begin working as individuals before working in pairs*. When you come to pairs work, the leader will have to be sensitive to the atmosphere and gauge how long to let each scene go on for. It is frustrating for a couple half-way through a good scene to be told to stop, but on the other hand, if ideas are slow in coming then it is good to change partners and situations frequently. Beware also of the temptation when in pairs to spend a lot of time talking about what you are going to do, and not enough time doing it.

To begin people working in pairs, get each group member to choose a character, a voice, a walk, and a particular hobby or interest for their character. Set them off walking round the room. At a given signal two characters meet and greet each other and they each try to interest the other in their particular obsession. Repeat the exercise with new characters.

By combining stock characters with stock situations you can develop many different scenes, with endless variations. Other situations you might use in pairs:

Interviews
    for a job
    with the doctor/therapist
    reporting an incident to the police
    opinion poll in street
    seeking practical help, e.g. applying for a grant, making a fortune, growing prize-winning marrows etc.
At a party
Travelling in a train
Reminiscing in old people's home

Dialogue on a park bench
In a waiting room
Carrying a large pane of glass in a busy street
Getting someone's head unstuck from railings

Always be on the look out, in your everyday life, for the situations that seem to provoke interesting transactions between two people, and try these out with your group.

**Stage 4
As a group**

From pairs you can progress to work in threes and fours and eventually to work involving the whole group. Try creating a scene in an hotel where each person has a different role and character: the nervous manager, a self-opinionated receptionist, a lazy doorman, and a variety of guests, from a scatterbrained old lady to a glamorous filmstar. Include a few objects such as an aspidistra, a crate of gin, a pistol and some money. Decide where the reception desk, front door, lift and rooms are and off you go! Let the situations develop with everyone being involved and literally see what happens. Put a time limit on this exercise — maybe ten minutes, longer if you wish — and set an alarm clock to go off when time is up.

Other variations for large group work could be: a party; on board an ocean liner; a factory; a public library; a public meeting or debate; a scene from the Bible — the disciples together; etc.

To improve creativity it often helps if you split into two smaller groups and prepare a scene to show to the others.

You must build up your own list of stock characters and situations. Use your own experience to the full. Pick up characters and situations from the Bible, from T.V., from songs, from local issues, from history.

**Sample session
General improvisation**

This is session 2 in the sample programme on page 13 and is intended as a general improvisation session.

1. Prayer — As in all sessions, begin by praying together. *5 minutes*

2. Warming up — Try and build on experience in previous sessions. Play the rhythm game, as you did in session 1, then play "Grandmother's Footsteps", or Charades, page 22. *20 minutes*

3. Park bench dialogue — Again building on experience in previous sessions:
○ Invite the group to recreate the park-bench dialogue they created in session 1 (page 28). *10 minutes*

○ Swap partners, but keep the same character as before and work out a new dialogue accordingly. *10 minutes*

○ Perform this second set of dialogues to one another, and choose among yourselves who you think the most interesting characters are. Put them to argue with each other, while the rest of you watch.

15 minutes

4. Situations   The previous exercise may have highlighted the weaknesses we discover when we try to "do" another character. This is because we often don't know our *own* reactions and habits, let alone begin to take on anyone else's. Explain how improvisation exercises help us first of all to get to know ourselves before we can get to know others.

○ Tell group members to find a space in the room where they are free to move around. They are now to play themselves in a number of situations:

trapped in a lift	*5 minutes*
failing their driving test	*5 minutes*
accidentally smashing a toilet at Buckingham Palace	*5 minutes*

○ Invite the group to pair off with one another. One now plays an interviewer, the other applying for a job — explaining why they think they are good for these particular jobs:

looking after the Queen's corgis	*5 minutes*
chairman of British Leyland	*5 minutes*

Swap around so that the other person then has a chance to sell themselves for the same jobs, or invent other jobs if you wish.

10 minutes

5. Feedback   Although you will not have produced any finished drama by the end of this session, you will have begun to experiment with different characters and situations which will build confidence and give your group experience to draw on. Spend the last few minutes of this session talking together about what you enjoyed, what you found easy, and what was difficult.

Sample session
Guided improvisation

This session takes a different approach to improvisation. It is designed to follow one specific theme — salesmen. Similar sessions could be developed about prisoners, snobbery, racism, preachers, politicians, children etc., according to what is important to your group at the time. This is session 4 in the sample programme on page 13.

1. Prayer   As in all sessions, begin by praying together.   *5 minutes*

2. Warming up   Get everyone on their feet and moving, having shed coats, shoes and socks. Play "Old King Cole" (see page 19) and follow it with some physical exercises as before, or a couple of energetic games such as "Stick in the Mud". *10 minutes*

3. Developing concentration

○ Give each person an object, e.g. a teapot, a spanner, a dog's lead, a telephone, a large mixing bowl. Get them to experiment with using their object in different ways, e.g. the teapot may become a trumpet, a magic lantern etc. Encourage people to talk to, as well as use, the object. Insist that they change its use every thirty seconds.

○ Get into pairs, deciding who is "A" and who is "B". Take it in turns to show each other some of the uses you have invented for your object. *10 minutes*

4. Developing ideas

○ Putting one of the objects aside, "A" and "B" invent new uses for the remaining object. Swap objects and repeat the exercise.

○ Each person takes their original object and decides on the most humorous, exciting or interesting use which has been invented for it, e.g. "A" may decide that his teapot is an ancient Egyptian vase once sealed in Tutankhamen's tomb. They then spend about a minute deciding on how they can best describe and show the qualities of their object in a lively, convincing argument.

○ "A" stands up and, imagining that he must sell his object, delivers one minute's convincing salesman's patter to his partner (who nevertheless must remain unconvinced, silent and impassive throughout), e.g. "This precious item, ladies and gentlemen, comes all the way from Ancient Egypt. A priceless piece of great mystery!" etc. "A" and "B" swap roles and repeat the exercise. *10 minutes*

5. Sharing ideas

○ Getting the whole group to sit down, tell one or two pairs to show the rest what they have developed.

○ After you have watched 4 or 6 "selling talks", ask the group if any of them have noticed the ways in which the stall-owner in the local market-place goes about his job, e.g. "Three for the price of two!" or "In London, ladies, they're flogging these for two quid! Now I'm not asking one seventy-five — I'm not even asking one-fifty. I don't want a pound! Tell you what, ladies, give me 50p!" Discuss ways in which market-sellers use their voice and their hands — especially clapping.

○ Put all the objects into the middle of the room and allow each person to choose a new one. Allow one minute for everyone to study it and think of a new selling approach. *15 minutes*

6. Developing ideas further

○ Send all the "A"s out of the room whilst the "B"s set out one chair each around the edges of the room. Tell the "B"s that they are salesmen, the room is a market-place and the chairs their stalls. They must stand on their chairs and "sell" their objects, competing for the attention of their audience of "A"s. Brief the "A"s so that they must stand in the middle of the room, moving towards whichever salesman seems the most interesting.

○ Change over roles and repeat the exercise — only this time tell the salesmen that they may have some awkward customers. Secretly arrange for one customer to be a heckler and for two others to ask continual questions about the product being sold.

○ Repeat a final time with the customers this time being definite characters. *15/20 minutes*

7. Using your ideas

You will most probably have run out of time by now, and this last important exercise might have to form the backbone of the next session rather than being rushed through at the end of this one. (If that is the case then spend time during the next session repeating some of the exercises you did in this session, and not rely on starting again from cold. Then go on to this next stage.)

○ Sit down and discuss what was good and why. Pick out not only selling techniques but also the way in which people respond to them. Try to isolate three or four very different responses.

○ In groups of four or five. One is a salesman who attempts to sell his wares to three or four different characters who respond in different ways to his approach. The last character actually buys the object — thus providing the end of the scene. *20/30 minutes*

You now have some basic material to work upon. A lot of this last session will have to be written off as gaining experience, and on the surface will not appear much use to you. But it will have added to your basic stock of resources. Changing the metaphor — it is like a steam engine where you need to build up sufficient power before you can begin to move. These sessions are building up the power to the point where you can actually create your own finished pieces of drama.

3. Bible study
Bible stories are presented very starkly. Your task is to develop their dramatic possibilities, and to find a manner of presentation that will be suitable to your audience.

Choosing a passage

Unless you have a specific request from your minister or someone else for a sketch on a particular theme or story, you are going to have to choose for yourself what parts of the Bible you are going to use. The main determinant will of course be subject, but be adventurous and experiment with various types of material.

Parables
Parables are the easiest material to work with. A parable always has a central message, and the drama should punch it home hard. Parables were told to a number of different audiences, e.g. to believers and unbelievers, so you should find one that is suitable to your audience. The most important thing about parables, however, is that they were intended to leave a memorable picture in the mind of the hearer, just as drama does, so dramatizing a parable is often simply a case of recreating that picture. A narrator, a son who has run away from home, some loose-livers, a jealous, resentful older brother, together create a picture. That picture can speak for itself — you seldom hear Jesus explaining his parables, ''You see the prodigal son is the Gentiles . . .'' — so allow the picture to remain in people's minds. (See the index to the Good News Bible, or page 665 of the Lion Handbook to the Bible, for lists of Old and New Testament Parables.)

Many of the simple scenes that appear in the parables are ideal situations for paired or group improvisation.

History/Biography *(The Gospels, Acts, Genesis, Exodus, Joshua to Esther)*
This writing provides you with anything from an epic with three hundred extras (Gideon in Judges chapters 6-8), to a simple conversation at a

well (John chapter 4), suitable for improvisation, or an extended story. Even spectacular events such as Moses parting the Red Sea can be represented through mime. Be careful not to rely too much on people knowing the story already — particularly a young audience. Choose stories and people whose theme is fairly easily transferable into our modern world, e.g. Joseph, the story of a young superstar surrounded by corruption, rather than a story such as that in the book of Ruth, which relies on an understanding of Middle Eastern rituals if it is to be properly communicated. But even these stories should not be written off. It is worth your while trying to understand them.

Law *(Exodus to Deuteronomy)*

This is about as easy to dramatize as a Civil Service Memorandum, and a lot of the teaching is re-expressed much more manageably in the New Testament by Jesus and by Paul. However, there are some stories, and particularly accounts of Israel's disobedience, that form valuable and relevant material for drama.

Poetry *(Job, Psalms and Songs of Songs)*

Poetry is best used in dance-drama, and in mime. Don't be fooled into thinking that dance is just long skirts and dainty gestures. In fact the border line between drama and dance is blurred. Dance is in fact dramatic movement, which can be a very effective accompaniment to the poetry of the Bible.

Wisdom and Prophets *(Proverbs, Ecclesiastes, Isaiah to Malachi, Revelation)*

These books only occasionally have a story running through them, though they do run parallel to the story told in the earlier books of the Old Testament. For dramatic purposes they offer hundreds of lenses which focus on various aspects of life (e.g. "Wealth is deceitful. Greedy men are proud and restless . . ." Habakkuk 2.5; and "Hot tempers cause arguments, but patience brings peace." Proverbs 15.18). Any one of these aspects could serve as the taking off point for a sketch, or the means of linking a number of different sketches around the same theme.

Letters *(Romans to Jude)*

Letters make up almost one third of the New Testament. They were written as personal communication between Christian leaders and various churches scattered around Asia and Europe, and did not therefore begin their lives as theology. If you can understand the problems behind the letters, you can develop drama which speaks to these problems. Additionally the Letters contain many images (e.g. buildings, races, weddings) which are used to describe the Christian life and can be the basis of a sketch.

Stories, People, Pictures

You will be looking for a story, a person or a picture, if a passage is to be immediately useful to you. As in previous sections it will most probably be of help to you if you build up lists of your own under the various headings, and indicate the passages to which the item relates or where it can be found.

The following lists are a starting point for you:

Stories	People	Pictures
N.T.		
Parables:	Simon Peter John 21	Slaves/freemen
Sheep and	Nicodemus John 3	Gal. 4
Goats Matt. 25	Pilate Luke 23	Race Phil. 3
Prodigal Son Luke 15	Barabbas Matt. 27	Light Matt. 5, 6
Wedding Feast	Ananias and	
Luke 14	Sapphira Acts 5	
O.T.		
Queen of Sheba's	Jonah	Measuring rod
visit to Solomon	Jeremiah	Ezekiel
1 Kings 10	Noah	Jealousy ⎤
Israel's religious		Anger ⎥ Proverbs
life 2 Chron. 31		Laziness ⎦
Calling Samuel		
1 Sam. 3		
David and Bathsheba		
2 Sam. 11		

Opt for passages which relate as closely as possible to day-to-day Christian life — e.g. temptation, loving others, witnessing, discipline etc.

There are many advantages also in working alongside what you or your church are reading or studying. This will enliven your own Bible study. It will probably give you a chance of performing in church. It will give you an outside perspective on the passage you are studying, rather than all the interpreting being left up to you. For an even more systematic approach you could follow a Bible Reading Plan, such as that put out by the Bible Society each year, and take a subject for a month or a fortnight, but beware of being too demanding and possibly discouraging your group.

**Sample session
Bible study**

As you dig into a passage you may discover that it says things that you did not expect. Be prepared for surprises! We often approach a passage as if it were a mirror, which reflects what we already think, rather than challenging us. So although the Bible may seem a little boring sometimes, take a second and third look, and try to see beyond your own prejudices.

You must also try to get the feel of the passage that you are studying. It is not just words. It is emotions. There are events behind it. There are people with personalities involved. Take the Parable of the Sower for instance. This was not delivered in the academic atmosphere of a lecture theatre, or a pulpit, or a synagogue, but from a boat, into which Jesus had been driven by the crush of a crowd. This should affect our understanding of the passage — Jesus was faced by a crowd who at that moment were completely absorbed by him, but what would they be like the next day? It also affects the context in which we might choose to perform the Parable of the Sower or some drama based on it. Where is there a similar, temporary absorption in Jesus?

This study of the Parable of the Sower is session 3 in the sample programme on page 13. This session is described more generally than other sample sessions, as we hope you will use it as a model for all Bible study sessions. Refer to the checksheets which follow on pages 43-48.

| 1. Prayer | As in all sessions, begin by praying together. | *5 minutes* |

1. Prayer As in all sessions, begin by praying together. *5 minutes*

2. Warming up Warming up is as important in this session as in the others. But always suit your warm-up to what is to follow — in this case aim at developing the group's concentration. Get the group to relax, sitting or lying down, with eyes closed. Pass a familiar item — e.g. cassette-box, pocket-stapler, apple — to one of the group members, and instruct them to describe it as fully as possible — but not to name it. e.g. It is round with a dimple at each end; it has a smooth surface . . . Get others to guess what it is. Repeat with other items. *10 minutes*

3. Recreating the passage You may wish just to read the passage. It will probably be more help, however, if you recreate the passage with a simple mime: a sower, four types of seed, and a narrator, each type of seed making appropriate noises — throttled, thirsty, eaten, growing — accompanied by actions. *10 minutes*

4. Discussing the background
Checksheet 1 (see page 43)

The leader of this session should have done work on this beforehand, and should use his or her discretion as to whether or not the group fills out the checksheets for themselves, as in some groups this may be off-putting and too much like "school". If everyone is doing it for themselves then each should find a space of their own in a corner of the room. After everyone has completed their sheet discuss the conclusions each has reached. You may find it helpful to stimulate your group with further questions about the background:

Who is presenting the message? What is so special about him or her? What can you find out about their background? How are they speaking? Harshly? In praise? In frustration? What was the speaker doing before this passage and after? Does it help explain the way he or she feels?

Who has recorded the message? e.g. Not only did Jesus *tell* this parable, but Matthew chose to *record* it. Why? What was his purpose in writing? Did he say, or can you discover who he was writing for? Who was this passage addressed to? i.e. If it was a story, who was in the crowd listening? If it was a letter, who was in the church it was addressed to? If it was a prophecy, who were the nation or group it was directed at? If it was a story, for whose benefit was it being recorded?

You should try to answer such questions as: Were the hearers Jews or Gentiles? Were they friends of the speaker? Had they heard this message before? Were they old or young, male or female? Are they listening as a group, or as individuals? Do they have noticeable faults or failings? Sometimes these questions cannot be answered from the evidence available to us, but those that can be answered help us to understand why the message is presented like it is, and who it might be appropriate to now. How is the message being presented? i.e. Is it a story, a biography, a letter, a speech, a conversation, a poem, a vision, a parable, a wise saying etc.? Why do you think this medium was chosen? *20 minutes*

5. Message
Checksheet 2 (see page 44)

This checksheet also helps you break down the story or passage into scenes or dramatic features which will be very useful to you in later improvisation exercises. Agree on the central message if you can, but allow each group member to contribute understandings which may be contradictory in the first place. Even having agreed on a message, your opinions may well be changed as you work on into checksheet 3. Encourage the group to be particularly adventurous about "headlines" as this may well throw up significant ideas as to how this passage may be presented. *20 minutes*

6. Audience
Checksheet 3 (see page 45)

Most of you will know already the kind of audience that will come to your performances. Discuss their interests. You might sometimes wish to work with a hypothetical audience in mind — a group who you think this passage might be appropriate for, but be realistic.

If you think you can find a group of non-Christian teenagers then seize the chance, but if you act in church, and just hope they will walk in, then think again. Be practical, and assess who you might have opportunity to perform for, and if you want to extend your audiences beyond that, consider what you must do to find new audiences. *10 minutes*

7. Meanings and equivalents
Checksheet 3

This is another exercise that will be of use to you in creating a script from this passage. First suggest a general significance for each of the items in the story, then, bearing in mind the audience you have opted for, complete the column "modern equivalents". You are looking for a person, a thing, an experience, a situation, or a command that would have the same effect on your new audience as the original person, thing, experience, situation, command etc. had on the original audience. Do not always opt for the most obvious equivalents. Spend time discussing possible equivalents. Bear in mind your stock of available characterizations built up in improvisation. You may be inaccurate to start with but stick at it. A problem is that most Christian drama relies on stereotypes. Simon Peter is presented by combining Geoff Capes (the shot putter) in size, Oliver Reed (the actor) in vigour, your local pentecostal pastor in enthusiasm, and whatever fishermen's qualities you observed when you holidayed in Cornwall. You build an identikit figure, not really a character. This may be inevitable, when a sketch is too short to allow the development of character, but *if it does worry you, try and develop longer scripts* in which character is allowed a gradual build-up. As long as you perform short sketches, you will find it hard to go beyond the "stereotype", which is only half the truth.

What you choose as the "major dramatic feature" on Checksheet 2 will set the scene for the rest of your drama, and particularly for the list of equivalents on Checksheet 3. If the sower is the major feature, then you must find the equivalent of the sower first (e.g. a salesman, a preacher, a farmer or a gardener), then the other equivalents will follow in the same mood (e.g. if you have chosen a salesman, then the places where the seed fell will be types of possible buyer).

Checksheets

Two sets of sample checksheets follow — the first relating to the sample session on the sower, the second relating to an Old Testament story.

42

Checksheet 1 "Background"

Passage:

MATTHEW 13. 1–9
(PARABLE OF THE SOWER)

From what book is this passage taken?	MATTHEW'S GOSPEL
Who wrote the book?	MATTHEW – JESUS' DISCIPLE/EX TAX COLLECTOR
Why did they write it?*	TO SHOW THAT JESUS WAS THE MESSIAH THE JEWS WERE WAITING FOR
Who did they write it to?*	JEWS

(*Refer to the introduction to each book in the Good News Bible)

What has happened just before this passage?	JESUS HAS 'REJECTED' HIS MOTHER AND BROTHERS (12.46)
What happens after it?	HE INTERPRETS THE SOWER ; TELLS MORE PARABLES AND THEN RETURNS TO NAZARETH, HIS HOME TOWN
Is it a parable/letter/history/other?	A PARABLE
Who are the audience/recipients?	CROWD OF BELIEVERS/UNBELIEVERS
Is it part of a series of passages with a particular purpose? If so, what purpose?	A SERIES OF STORIES, EVENTS AND PARABLES INDICATING WHAT THE KINGDOM OF GOD IS LIKE

Checksheet 2 "Message"

Passage: **MATTHEW 13.1-9**

Dramatic features or scenes:

1. THRONGING CROWD – JESUS GETS INTO A BOAT
2. JESUS TELLS STORY
3. SOWER GOES OUT
4. SEED ON PATH – BIRDS EAT IT
5. SEED ON ROCK – SUN SCORCHES IT
6. SEED IN THORNS – THROTTLED
7. SEED IN GOOD SOIL – MULTIPLIES
8. WARNING TO LISTEN AND LEARN

Major dramatic feature(s):

1. SOWER
2. FRUITFUL SEED

How will a modern version help, if at all?

GIVE THIS FAMILIAR STORY NEW IMPACT

Choose a headline for the passage:

ONLY A FEW SURVIVE

In two sentences, put the message in your own words:

MAN HAS THE OPPORTUNITY TO BE WHAT
GOD WANTS US TO BE. BUT SOMETIMES OUR
LIVES ARE SO FULL OF DISTRACTIONS (SIN?)
THAT GOD CANNOT GET A LASTING
INFLUENCE ON US.

Checksheet 3 "Meanings and equivalents"

Passage:

MATTHEW 13. 1-9

Describe audience: CONGREGATION ON SUNDAY MORNING AT OUR CHURCH. MULTI-RACIAL. FAMILY SERVICE. EASILY BORED. KNOW 'SOWER' QUITE WELL ALREADY.

In the passage	General meaning	Modern equivalents
Major dramatic feature(s): SOWER FRUITFUL SEED	COMMON OCCUPATION FULFILLED POTENTIAL	SALESMAN BUYER
People: LISTENERS DISCIPLES	ENQUIRING PEOPLE KEEN FOLLOWERS	LIKELY BUYERS CONVINCED CONSUMERS
Places: LAKE SIDE	COMMON MEETING PLACE	AT FRONT DOOR/ IN THE STREET
Symbols/pictures/rituals: PATH ROCKY GROUND THORNS GOOD SOIL BIRDS SUN	WELL-WORN GROUND UNDERNOURISHED GROUND OVERCROWDED GROUND IDEAL GROUND COMMON HAZARD COMMON HAZARD	DISINTEREST SHALLOW INTEREST DISTRACTION SUCCESSFUL SALE } DISTRACTIONS

Checksheet 1 "Background"

Passage:

2 KINGS 5.1-27
(THE CURE OF NAAMAN)

From what book is this passage taken?	2 KINGS
Who wrote the book?	?
Why did they write it?*	TO SHOW HOW THE DESTRUCTION OF JERUSALEM WAS AN INEVITABLE RESULT OF GODLESSNESS
Who did they write it to?*	A HISTORY BOOK FOR THE JEWS

(*Refer to the introduction to each book in the Good News Bible)

What has happened just before this passage?	ELISHA HAS PERFORMED MIRACLES
What happens after it?	ELISHA PERFORMS FURTHER MIRACLES
Is it a parable/letter/history/other?	A STORY
Who are the audience/recipients?	JEWS
Is it part of a series of passages with a particular purpose? If so, what purpose?	THE SERIES OF MIRACLES SEEMS TO ILLUSTRATE THE POWER OF THE TRUE MAN OF GOD

Checksheet 2 "Message"

Passage:

2 KINGS 5.1-27

Dramatic features or scenes:

1. NAAMAN HEARS OF ELISHA FROM SERVANT
2. NAAMAN GETS PERMISSION FROM KING TO GO
3. NAAMAN IS TOLD BY ELISHA TO WASH IN JORDAN
4. NAAMAN FIRST REFUSES THEN PERSUADED TO WASH
5. NAAMAN BELIEVES AND OFFERS ELISHA GIFTS
6. SERVANT CHEATS NAAMAN
7. SERVANT GETS THE DISEASE

Major dramatic feature(s):

1. WASHING IN JORDAN
2. LEPROSY

How will a modern version help, if at all?

A MODERN VERSION MIGHT BE TOO 'STRAINED' — MUST FIND A GOOD EQUIVALENT OF 'JORDAN'

Choose a headline for the passage:

DO EXACTLY AS GOD SAYS

In two sentences, put the message in your own words:

GOD REWARDS YOU ACCORDING TO YOUR OBEDIENCE NOT THE SPLENDOUR OF YOUR RITUAL. GOD CAN GIVE PHYSICAL HEALING IF YOU TRULY OBEY HIM.

Checksheet 3 "Meanings and equivalents"

Passage:

2 KINGS 5. 1-27

Describe audience: SUNDAY EVENING YOUTH SERVICE. CONGREGATION MAINLY YOUNG ADULTS. A LOT OF THEM ARE TURNED-OFF THE OLD TESTAMENT

In the passage	General meaning	Modern equivalents
Major dramatic feature(s):		
WASHING IN JORDAN	SIMPLE RITUAL	PRAYING
LEPROSY	DREADED DISEASE	CANCER
People: NAAMAN	GOOD MAN-WRONG SIDE	NICE MUSLIM
ELISHA	GOOD MAN-RIGHT SIDE	HOLY CHRISTIAN
KINGS-SYRIA/ISRAEL	POLITICIANS	AYATOLLAH/PRIME MINISTER
SERVANT GIRL	NEWS-BRINGER	NEWSPAPER
OTHER SERVANTS	COMMON SENSE	COMMON SENSE
GEHAZI	GRASPING/IMMORAL MAN	COMMERCIAL EXPLOITER
Places:		
ELISHA'S HOUSE	HOME OF HOLY MAN	VICARAGE
RIVER JORDAN	SYMBOL OF STATE RELIGION	SUBURBAN ANGLICAN CHURCH
TEMPLE OF RIMMON	SYMBOL OF CONFLICTING RELIGION	REGENTS PARK MOSQUE
Symbols/pictures/rituals:		
GIVING GIFTS	COMMON RITUAL	CONFERRING HONOURS

3

Presenting and Performing

1. Making a script

By now you will have built up and be happy with some basic situations and characters. You will have built up a picture of the passage you are working with. You now need to add them together to create drama.

But it is not that simple. If it was, then successful dramatists would not be so rare. In fact we can only help you to a limited extent, because now *it is up to you* as an individual or as a group to feed the creative spark.

There is one important principle: *remember your audience and how best to communicate with them*. Suit your manner of presentation to the audience, or the preacher you are backing. You will need to be more concerned about blending drama in with what already exists in the life of your church, group, or organization, than indulging every flight of fancy, or fantasy that comes to mind. Remember, audiences are more than just "kids" or "church", they are types of kids, types of churches. They have ages, backgrounds, levels of understanding.

It may help if you think of yourselves as *Bible translators*. You are taking words and concepts that not many people understand and translating them into actions that most people can understand. Only about 40% of people in England regularly read books. That leaves 60% who might watch or listen to films, music and plays, but for whom the Bible would be a closed book, because all books are closed books. This means that clarity is more important than cleverness.

Choosing a style

There are many different styles you might use in your drama.
○ We are all familiar with *traditional Bible drama,* as used at Sunday School Anniversaries and primary school nativity plays. With an old dressing gown and a towel on your head you pass as Jesus, Simon Peter, Judas or Zacchaeus. Do not write this off. It is particularly appropriate for New Testament stories, but recognize its limitations. For a lot of people it has negative connotations, and is sometimes thought of as childish or patronizing.
○ *Dance-drama* is well accepted in many churches, sometimes where other drama is not. It is a highly specialized form of communication, with immense potential, and we have not had space to cover it in this book. It can be a highly dramatic means of presenting the Bible and particularly of symbolizing events and concepts that might be quite strained in other drama, e.g. the creation story, visionary writings, etc.
○ *Mime* should become one of your stocks-in-trade. An effective mime

can often simulate an inanimate object, an event, a character, a personality, or a complicated action, more easily than scenery, dialogue, or busy activity. If using mime plus narration, however, ensure that the mime or the action is as well thought out as the narration. Good drama demands that the focus be upon the mime, not on the narrator. The narration must appear as a commentary on the action, not vice versa.

○ *Narration* can serve as an introduction, a link or a comedy device. It should never serve as an excuse for bad communication. What is the point of the drama if no one knows what you are doing or saying until the narrator tells them? Having said that, however, narration is a highly adaptable device. It offers original viewpoints — the Good Samaritan

can be narrated from the viewpoint of any of the characters in it, an impartial observer, a wayside rock, a news reporter etc. Narration offers a scene-setting device — ''There were once ten Liverpool F.C. supporters, five wise and five foolish . . .'' One narrator can be played off against another to add comic effect, or pace (see A Tale of Two Men page 83). Narrators can be equally involved in the action of a piece of drama.

○ *Styles from the mass media.* There are literally hundreds of available styles from the media that can form the setting for a sketch: sports commentators, panel games, quiz games, current affairs programmes, pantomime, magazine programmes, phone-ins, American detective/cowboy series, documentary, news reports. Always be on the look out for situations you can use, e.g. Could Nicodemus phone Jesus on a phone-in, rather than ''coming by night''? — it is equally anonymous.

○ At a more simple level you can tell *a Bible story with modern equivalents* substituted for the original components.

○ There are certain *everyday events* that can be developed for effective drama: park-bench, or garden-fence dialogues; classroom arguments; queues in employment exchange; commuters on British Rail etc. T.V. comedians such as John Cleese, or Peter Cooke have made the most of such material.

○ Notice if you can how the Bible fits into people's lives: they read it from a poster; a friend quotes it; they hear a sermon; they read it themselves; they remember a childhood song; they watch the T.V. religious spot. Develop an everyday scene in which the Bible speaks quite naturally.

○ Use melodrama, absurd situations, historical events etc. to give your drama variety.

○ In choosing a style, look at the Bible itself. It contains many forms of writing and communication, and different forms were chosen for different audiences — a poem, or a piece of street theatre (Jeremiah), or a parable, or a chant, or a vision etc. They were the contemporary media, and in order to communicate, the people who spoke on God's behalf, and God himself, chose *from the available media* a form which would get home to their listeners.

Hints on writing

Nothing is easier to write than bad drama. Good writing requires practice. Before you begin it is a good idea for you to study other examples of writing — see the Bibliography — and discover what you think is a good style of writing. The following hints may help you:

○ You cannot write a script by committee, so if you have more than one member who wants to try their hand, then each person should do so separately and then pool ideas, or the group should try out all the different scripts. Feedback is important. Damaging criticism should be avoided, but honest opinions should be expressed constructively. Always treat all material, written or improvised, as work in progress, until it has been given a thorough testing by yourself and observers.

○ Be consistent in your use of one style per script: it's a fine art to mix both slapstick and serious drama.

○ A script must move *fast and rhythmically,* so that any change in pace, a sudden stop or change to slow motion will be obvious and effective.

○ Work within the capabilities of your group, gradually stretching them. Use characters which your group has proved to be good at in improvisation.

○ Concentrate on beginnings and endings, as they will set the pace for the middle.

○ Don't make dialogue too clever or involved. Allow complexities to emerge during improvisation.

○ Perform what you are writing as you go along, to iron out verbal trip-wires.

○ Keep your audience central in your mind at all times.

○ Use the list of modern equivalents that you have prepared on Checksheet 3. It will help you, not just in choice of setting and style, but in characterization, plot and language.

○ Discover what styles and settings are most likely to interest and provoke your audience, then choose accordingly.

○ Create opposites in the action, e.g. Mr. Good and Mr. Evil, not Mr. Normal and Mr. Average. This is often done in Bible teaching.

○ Choose definite characterizations — even in short scripts — not just a wise man, but a wise man from Cambridge, B.A. Hons (1st Class) architecture (see The Two Builders page 73).

○ Do not *always* rely on ''humour'', but recognize that it is probably the most immediate of the styles available to you.

○ Even if you are writing a script it will take you a long time to reach the finished article, so consider it to be work in progress as always. When the group try it out, cut out excess dialogue, notice your visual effect, develop strong beginnings and endings, all the time realizing that writing is a continuous process.

In creating Bible drama, you will come across one unavoidable difficulty — that is, how to represent Jesus or God. Jesus, as God incarnate, is not just another holy man. It is often difficult to find an adequately respectful representation of Jesus the Son of God, and therefore of some of the events in his ministry.

These are some of the ways we have so far found to do this:

○ We believe that Jesus is alive and currently with us, so it is not a cop-out to introduce Jesus in person to the modern situation just as he appeared in person in the original story.

○ Some of the things that Jesus did on earth have now become, at Jesus' wish, the responsibilities of "the church" which is described as the Body of Christ. So it is quite acceptable to choose, for instance, a church leader as the agent of healing, if you have decided to keep healing as an element of your version of one of Jesus' healing miracles.

○ The teaching ministry of Jesus and some of the early church fathers has, to a great degree, been taken on by the Bible. And so, where it is possible, introduce the Bible as the instrument of change in, for instance, the experience of the rich young ruler.

○ Finally, although in some cases the most important factor in a story from Jesus' life is the event itself, in others it is how people responded and how Jesus responded as a human being. It is in fact the reactions and emotions involved that are important. So Footprints have represented Jesus as "a nice guy", as a carpenter with supernatural power, once as a school caretaker, sometimes as a hero of a particular social group. But you must be sensitive in this area and not pretend that "anything goes". Christian drama is still quite new for a lot of people, and it is foolish to make it offend anyone unnecessarily.

If you want further ideas of how various dramatic techniques can be used, look at the sketches at the end of this book. See how the narrator is used. See how humour is used. Notice rhyme and rhythm. Notice length, level of language and the speed at which a sketch moves. Watch other drama groups in action.

For further guidance, go to the theatre. Watch professionals. Watch T.V. drama. In this area as much as anywhere, you need to observe others and the way they do things, and incorporate what you learn into your own work.

Writing through improvisation

Even if you cannot write, all is not lost. We have been emphasizing all along that improvisation is a substitute for script-writing, and the exercises in the Bible study sessions are all designed to make this easier. Recap on the sample sessions on pages 32-35, and consider how the two can be brought together. Incidentally we did not do those sessions in the order you might have expected. We had used a version of the "salesman" session two or three weeks before coming to the "Parable of the Sower", but the remarkable way they interlocked is an example of the way improvisation can provide you with the very material you need for creating Bible sketches.

Whatever material you are working from, be it a Bible story, or a story developed from a Bible theme etc., one of the first things to do is to study a breakdown of the story into recognizable scenes as on Checksheet 2. When working on Matthew 13. 1-9 for "Special Offer" (page 44) we broke the story down like this:

1. Sower goes out and scatters seed.
2. Seed falls on pathway, birds soon eat it.
3. Seed falls on rocky ground, takes root but withers in sun.
4. Seed falls in thorn bushes which choke it.
5. Seed falls on good soil and produces corn.
6. Warning to take notice.

Working from the ideas and characters developed in the "salesman" session we worked out a series of equivalents like this:

1. A salesman offers his product.
2. A posh woman rejects it with no sign of interest.
3. A hippie tries it briefly, but is soon put off.
4. A worried man has no time to sample product.
5. A young man, tries it, likes it, and shares it with others.
6. The salesman emphasizes the importance of accepting his product.

The next stage is to discuss *very* briefly the situations and characters involved and the point you wish to make, and to decide on a particular style or setting for the piece which will help to direct everyone's ideas towards a unified end-product.

The work we did on salesman's patter in the sample session, for example, suggested the use of a lot of rhyme and rhythm in working out "Special Offer": the four very different characters involved in the story created an image of a row of houses on a street and this led naturally to our salesman becoming a door-to-door salesman.

Don't worry if you cannot see all the characters or stages clearly in your mind at this point. Take one or two of the scenes for which you have the most ideas and have a go at improvising them. Working in small groups you can produce more than one version from which you can select the best idea to develop. This should spark off further ideas for how to tackle the other, perhaps more difficult, stages of the story.

Improvise each scene separately, keeping each piece as short as possible, always remembering that eventually you will want to put them together to make a dramatically unified and interesting whole.

When you watch each other's improvisations, learn to say more than just "That was good", or "I liked that". Apart from mildly encouraging the actors, comments like these will not help your work to grow and improve. Without being too destructive, try to analyse what has been performed and discuss what could be improved, e.g. "It would have been better if the hippie tasted the banana without peeling it".

Brief the group to look out for particular things such as mime skills, aspects of staging or the clever use of words. Always regard the sharing of improvised scenes as experiment so that people do not feel under great pressure to perform masterful works of art every time scenes are viewed by the group.

One more golden rule: be adventurous, and never be afraid of failure when you are experimenting with ideas. Every idea that goes wrong, every slip-up or weak piece of work, can still be a useful experience as you learn from your mistakes. Very often the idea or sketch which is the hardest to get right turns out to be the most effective when you finally perform it.

If you feel that you must have a script, then later on, when you have run through a scene over and over again to the point where you are satisfied with it, use a cassette tape recorder to record a run-through of it.

This will serve two major purposes:
○ It will help you to criticize what you have done, e.g. does any of it sound garbled or stilted?
○ With a little patience one of you can transcribe the recording on to paper — perhaps working on the resulting script to improve weak dialogue etc.

A word of warning though: never be too hasty to record something or write it down. It is much better to run through an improvised scene over and over again, with another member of the group watching to give criticism and to eventually act as director. The Footprints sketches in this book were not written down until they had been performed about seventy times.

2. Shaping your presentation

You can't please all of the people all of the time, so until you have the experience and confidence as a group to face possible criticism philosophically and to learn from your mistakes, don't try anything too adventurous. Start off by performing simple things which use your particular strengths as a group and have a clear, basic message. If, for example, some of you already have confidence in using music or singing in church, then base your first piece of work on that experience, and build quite a lot of music into your performance. Always begin with

what you already know you can do well. This will build up your confidence and your reputation.

Beginnings and endings

Whether you are performing a short sketch or a full length epic you should stick to the old formula of giving it an obvious beginning, an interesting middle, and a definite end!

Although anti-climaxes and highly atmospheric beginnings and endings can be used very effectively by experienced groups, they require considerable skill. It is usually better to give your drama too much "punch" and definition, leaving your audience in no doubt as to how to respond, rather than trying to be too subtle and making them feel uncomfortable or confused.

Pace and variety

If you are presenting a series of sketches, vary the number of actors from one to the next, use different dramatic styles side by side and try to vary the moods in the different parts of the presentation, e.g. narration and mime followed by a musical sketch. Similarly when constructing a longer play, try to give it variety and texture by placing a lively colourful scene next to a quieter more meditative one.

Conventions

You may be familiar with the techniques used by television and film-makers to create particular effects, e.g. the rippling of the screen to signify a flashback or the fading of the picture to show a change of scene etc. These techniques are known as conventions, and some of them can be used in drama.

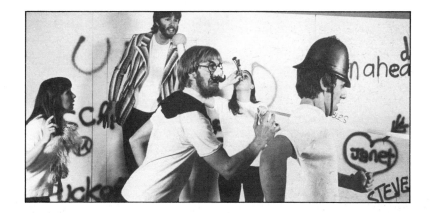

The freeze
This is when a character, or several characters, suddenly stop. It is a dramatic moment: it commands the audience's attention, and is an effective way of ending a sketch, of concentrating the audience's attention on the words of a narrator, or of showing the passing of time. Another way of using a freeze is where a scene suddenly stops, and one of the characters steps out of the situation to address the audience. As he steps back into the scene the other characters come to life again as if nothing has happened. If a group of people are to "freeze" together then they should be given some kind of definite signal to ensure that they all start moving again at exactly the same moment, otherwise the scene will look ragged and the effectiveness of the freeze will be lost.

Slow motion

To move properly in slow motion requires much physical discipline and control, as it acts to focus an audience's attention on the detail of movement. It can be very effective when used together with a narration spoken at normal speed, or to contrast one character against others who are moving faster, e.g. a starving beggar on a busy city street.

Turning your back to the audience

Actors used to be told never to turn their backs to an audience but this convention is a widely practised and most useful one in contemporary drama. If a character stands quite still with his back to the audience, he will become unnoticed as other action takes place in the acting area. Standing in this particular position can be a substitute for ''going off-stage'' in certain styles of presentation, or when exits and entrances are difficult or impossible to arrange. You can also use the convention of standing frozen with your back to the audience as a way of signifying that an actor is going to become a different character when he or she turns around and joins in the action again.

Using the body to represent an object

It is amazing what an audience can be made to believe in if the actors do their job well. Two actors kneeling down with arms outstretched horizontally will soon be accepted as a market trader's stall once the imaginary scales standing on it are used. An audience will soon forget that the railway signal which stops the express train just in time is really a person standing very straight and stiff, using simple arm movements. If the object you want to represent is to remain inanimate (not a living thing) then the actor must try to really believe that he is that object, and he must take on all of its qualities. Once he begins to show any human qualities, e.g. facial expressions, then the object will come to life — although this may occasionally be the desired effect, e.g. the tree which tells the story of a man called Zacchaeus who climbed up it to see an important person passing.

Experiment with different ways of using actors to create certain effects. Once you manage to get the audience involved in the story of your drama, their imaginations will do most of the work for you.

If your performance consists of several short sketches making a series of different points, then it may be necessary to provide a way of helping the audience to follow the thought process through.

One person could act as a kind of compere, saying a few words

Links

between each sketch to link one to the next. If you use this method, however, he or she should beware of repeating the message of what has gone before or giving away the point of what is to follow. These links do not always have to be done by the same person, nor do they have to be in the form of a "straight" spoken piece. Sketches can be linked by poems, songs or even by a character who pops up now and then to provide comment on the action — you could even use silent-movie type captions.

Whatever your sketches and however the ideas have been linked, the audience must be able to feel at the end of it that it has all made sense. Sometimes you may wish to leave the audience wondering what one or two of the sketches were getting at, but whatever you do — never leave them wondering what *all* the sketches were trying to say!

Tools of the trade

No matter how simple your drama is going to be, there are three basic "tools of the trade" which you will find yourself using in some shape or form.

A set

This means any background which you provide for your action, as well as the "furniture" you may use to sit on, stand on, or jump over. The set should be as simple as possible, because quite apart from the fact that you will probably have to put the set up and down several times in different places, you will find that large painted scenery with blue lagoons and potted palms will probably only serve to distract your audience from what really matters — the actors! Any scenery you

have will also need to be adaptable for different situations and different pieces of drama. A couple of easily portable screens would probably be the best investment, as they can be used not only for changing behind and providing easy entrances and exits for the actors, but they will also provide a plain and simple backcloth when you are asked to perform in front of a complicated or distracting background — such as that which the front of many churches offer. If a particular piece of drama demands that a certain design is painted onto your screens, then plain coloured drapes (curtains) can be used to cover them on the occasions when the design is not considered suitable or necessary.

If you perform frequently in different places and you have the right sort of transport facilities, you may find it useful to carry around a few simple stage blocks or rostra. These are low, small platform-like blocks with which you can build small raised areas in places where visibility is a problem, or to give added variety and interest. Other things which you may find useful, and very adaptable, are a pair of brightly painted step ladders, a free-standing door, a set of painted chairs, a hat stand, or a selection of different coloured wooden cubes. A pair of step ladders can become a pulpit, the commentator's box at a race meeting, or the watchtower of a castle.

Properties (or "props")

These are the things which the actors use whilst performing, e.g. walking-sticks, handkerchiefs, buckets and spades etc. Use as few props as possible, and make them very simple. Props are often more of a hindrance than a help in situations where the same ideas could have been conveyed much more effectively by the use of mime, e.g. telephones, bicycles etc. If props get lost or forgotten, or even just left in the wrong place on the set, it can cause great confusion. Because of this it is best to appoint someone to be in charge of them. They can then keep a list of which props are needed for each play or sketch and should remember where they should be placed before the performance begins. (It is also advisable that each actor checks that his own personal props are where they should be prior to the performance.)

Costume

Biblical costume with old dressing gowns and towel-covered heads are what many people immediately think of at the mention of dramatized Bible stories. For this very reason it is best to avoid attempts at recreating biblical costume unless it is for a particular reason, for very young children, or to make a comical point. Modern dress or a timeless costume which does not suggest any particular era are often far more effective for a modern audience who will find it easier to identify with someone who dresses as they do, rather than someone who looks as if they have stepped out of a history book.

Most groups find it best to have a basic, simple costume which all the members wear, such as jeans or trousers with T-shirts, sweat shirts or plain jumpers in the same or a contrasting colour. These can then be supplemented by easily added pieces of costume like hats, waistcoats, aprons, scarves etc. which suggest the character the actor is playing at any one time.

Sometimes, however, you may find that you want to have full costume for a particular play or character. As this can be very expensive it is a good idea to buy cheap lengths of material from markets, and to keep your eyes open for unusual and interesting items of clothing in second-hand shops and at jumble sales.

3. Preparing for a performance

The rehearsal schedule

Once a date has been set for the first performance of a piece it is up to the leader of the group to work out a rough rehearsal schedule. This means starting from the date of the performance and working backwards through the time available; planning a dress rehearsal, a technical run-through (when any lighting, sound, music etc. is fitted into the programme); a date by which all lines should have been learnt and time for the actors to develop their characters etc.

The role of the director

The role of the director can be taken either by the group leader, or a group member. The director's job is to be an outside eye. As he is not usually involved in the action he can see the drama as the audience will see it, judging not only the individual parts of the play but also the overall effect. This means that although the actors should be free to contribute their own ideas, the director should always have the last word. He should expect quietness and discipline in rehearsals.

The director needs to be sensitive to the moods and feelings of the group, both individually and as a whole. Criticisms should always be constructive. If the group as a whole seems bored or are fooling around when the director wants to work on something serious, then he should get back their interest or let them work off excess excitement by playing some games, or working on a comedy situation, which will eventually lead back into the work that he really wants to tackle.

Interpreting a script

Staging

A good script will not try to give you too many complicated stage directions, but will give basic positions where different events should take place, and leave decisions about detail to the individual group or director. These basic positions are usually given in the form of the following technical abbreviations:

Stage Right (S.R.)
Stage Left (S.L.) — The right or left side of the acting area as seen by the actor looking towards the audience.

Downstage (D.S.) — The front of the acting area (nearest to the audience).

Upstage (U.S.) — The back of the acting area.

Obviously it is up to you to decide how you can make the piece visually effective. The actors should be positioned so that the audience has maximum visibility. The acting area should never appear cluttered, unless that is the effect desired, and it should always be clear to the audience which character or characters their attention should be focused on at any one time. For this reason the director should look out for any actor who "upstages" the main action, i.e. attracts undue attention to himself at the other performers' expense.

Atmosphere

In order to deal with this as practically as possible, we have written this section with reference to "The Story of Little Billy and Big Joe" (page 77). So, if you haven't already done so, you will need to read the sketch before going any further. As you read it ask yourself basic questions such as: What sort of atmosphere prevails in this scene? Are the characters realistic or are they intended to be caricatures and larger than life? How do I see this happening on a stage?

Voice

After reading the script you will realize that all the characters have American accents. Before trying to "learn the lines", study an American television programme and copy an accent. Practise speaking in that accent, make a tape-recording and listen to it. Does it sound authentic? Better still, if you know an American, get them to help you. Throughout the script the actors have to make various motorcycle sound effects. Go into a busy street and tape-record some motorbikes, then imitate the noises.

Mime

Big Joe, the girls and Little Billy all mime riding on motorcycles. If you don't ride a motorbike yourself then find a friend who will let you

practise sitting on his bike and show you how to operate the controls. Transfer this groundwork to the discipline of mime. In front of a full length mirror, mount and sit on an imaginary bike. Get someone to guess what you are doing. If your mime is effective they should guess within three seconds. There is no substitute for practice in making mime convincing. How does Big Joe move around on his bike? Develop a method of moving around whilst still convincing your audience that you are on a motorbike. There is a lot of movement involved in the sketch, and it is the comedy of this which provides much of its appeal.

Characters

Obviously in casting the sketch you need to take into consideration build and looks, but it is not enough for an actor to look like Big Joe: for the time when the sketch is being performed he must *become* Big Joe. Ask basic questions about each character. What does Big Joe do when he is not meeting up with Little Billy? How did he earn the reputation of being "rough and tough"? How old is Little Billy at each stage in the story? What other things does he enjoy doing? Has he ever had a girl friend before?

The characters have a whole life outside the sketch — the sketch simply uncovers and portrays a few minutes or hours out of their lives. Perhaps through improvisation you could imagine Townsville, some of the other inhabitants and some of the other things which happen there. All this work will help to make the final polished performance richer and more interesting for both actors and audience.

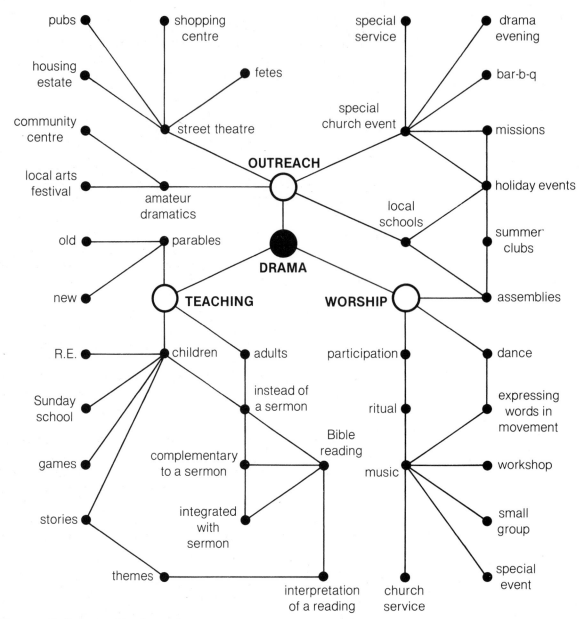

Diagram 2: Opportunities for performance

4. Opportunities for performance

Diagram 2 shows the many possibilities for performing. You will be able to add to it. You will probably have three main openings, however: church services, street theatre or special events.

Church services

Fitting in

Be sensitive to the atmosphere of worship which most people expect in a church service. This will vary from church to church and will also depend on whether the service is in the morning or evening, and on the age group of the congregation. A general rule is *simplicity*. Keep to your allotted time and try to use as few costumes and props etc. as possible, in order to cut down on the fuss you need to make when it is time for your contribution to the worship. In some churches there is sufficient freedom for the congregation to applaud at the end of your performance and to feel uninhibited if you request any kind of involvement, but you cannot presume either of these unless you know the particular situation well.

What to do

There are two main types of contribution you can make to a church service. One is obviously that of teaching — with lively sketches, dramatized readings and songs, which will be particularly relevant to a family service. The other is that of actually leading the congregation in worship, presenting more meditative pieces perhaps involving dance or movement. This second use of drama is perhaps most effective in evening services with a mainly adult congregation.

Planning ahead

If you are contributing to a service which is being led by someone else, it is important to liaise with them beforehand so that what you do will be complementary to what they have planned. Many preachers have a nasty habit of either apparently ignoring what the drama has said, by not even mentioning it in the following sermon or talk, or of taking away its impact by going over the same ground again, making your carefully prepared message seem laboured and driven home with a sledge hammer.

Practical problems

On the practical level, churches are not designed for theatrical presentations. You may find that you have very little space, and what little there is may be cluttered with various items of furniture. Try to get as much of this furniture cleared away as you can without upsetting or

65

offending anyone, and then make the best use of what you are left with. You could have some of the action happening in the aisle, for example, or put the narrator up in the pulpit. Do not let a strange-shaped acting area limit you — use its features to make what you do more effective for the audience.

Remember that big, old churches often have bad acoustics, and remind your actors that the old lady on the back row may be deaf! If careful diction and well-projected voices still fail to make her sit up and take notice, then you may have to plan your drama around whatever public address system the church has installed.

Use recorded sound, music or a narrator standing at a microphone to provide the main source of sound with most of the action as mime.

Street theatre

How

There are four main ways of using street theatre in evangelism and outreach.

○ Where you simply present the Gospel message through the performance and hope that your witness will set people thinking and searching for more.

○ Where you encourage the audience to engage in personal conversation with the actors at the end of the performance.

○ Where you hand out Christian literature to the crowd attracted by the drama. Wherever possible such literature should have an obvious connection with what is being performed either through its design and approach or through its actual content.

○ Where the drama is used as publicity for some other performance or meeting, such as a crusade or mission, which is happening that, or the next, day.

Where

The spot you choose to perform can make a big difference. You obviously need a large enough space to perform, but also remember that there needs to be room for your audience to gather without blocking footpaths, shop doorways, or spilling over onto roads. Unless your performance is designed to be "in-the-round" try to find somewhere which provides a natural backdrop — a wall, a building, a fence, a statue or memorial or a flight of steps can all make good settings for street theatre.

Choose a site where people would normally congregate, such as a town square with park benches, a seaside promenade or a busy shopping centre. But beware — many shopping arcades and precincts are privately owned and you will soon have irate shop owners after you for distracting potential customers and blocking the view of their window display. During school holidays parks, playgrounds and open spaces on housing estates can be very fruitful ground if you have material designed particularly for children. Wherever you decide to perform, it is always best to seek police permission, as a responsible attitude towards such things should be part of the witness of your group. They usually require at least two weeks' notice.

What

First make your presence and your intention to perform very obvious. Make a lot of noise and a lot of fuss. You could have someone with a loud voice announcing from the top of a pair of step ladders who you are and what is about to happen, whilst others blow hooters, bang drums and generally make their presence known. No matter how much noise you make, however, your real audience will not gather until you actually start performing something. This means that the first few minutes of what you do can afford to be concerned with "throwaway" humour, and certainly should not contain anything vital to the plot or your message.

If the weather is cool, or if you are in a place where people tend to pass through rather than hang around, then the best format to adopt is a continuous programme of short sketches lasting a maximum of four or five minutes each. The shorter and more to the point each sketch is the better. If you are performing on a warm, sunny day, in a spot where people will happily sit or stand around to be entertained (such as in a park or on a beach), then you can present a longer street play consisting of several scenes — being careful not to let your audience's attention wander by linking the scenes with a lively narration or live music.

On the whole, the most suitable style of presentation for street work seems to be that where clever word-play (rhyme, rhythm, alliteration and puns) is left to one or two characters who have strong voices and can relate directly to the audience, with the rest of the actors providing the action and visual interest.

Style

Whatever else street theatre is, it is not subtle. What you do needs to be big, live, loud and colourful. Costumes should be bright and outlandish, props comical and oversized. Most of your material needs to be funny,

even slapstick. Theatre outdoors is entertainment with a capital E. If your audience is not entertained they will not just be bored, they will be non-existent!

Back-up
Bible Society produces scripture selections that can be used with all ages. These can be overprinted by you and made specific to your audience. (See Bibliography.) You could also design your own handout to fit in with the themes of the drama.

Special events

Why bother?
Organizing a special event where people come along especially to see your performance means a lot of extra work for a group, but it really is

worth the effort. You will have far less trouble persuading non-Christian friends to come to a performance than you would have getting them to a church service or evangelistic meeting. If it is well advertized locally you may find that you attract some complete outsiders — although this is more likely to happen if you use a village, town, or school hall rather than your own church hall which will put off those who automatically assume that "Christian" means boring!

The main advantage of an event like this is that you have more freedom to develop your own ideas and style than you have when performing in church services. You are able to be more lively and humorous than you would be in church, and more subtle and sensitive to your audience than in street theatre. By the use of humour you can soon create a relaxed atmosphere, winning over your audience and making them surprisingly open to the message you convey through your drama.

If the hall you use has a stage, you do not necessarily have to use it. It will often make your drama, and your relationship with an audience, more immediate and intimate if you perform on floor level and closer to them than a platform will allow. Try arranging the audience on two or three sides of the action, or all the way round with the action in the middle. Have characters popping up and entering from unexpected places, perhaps from the back of the audience or even from the audience itself.

Planning the programme

It takes quite a lot of material to fill a programme of about an hour, which is really the shortest amount of time for which you can justifiably gather an audience. The performance could consist of one full-length play, two or three playlets of twenty or thirty minutes each, or it could be made up of various shorter sketches, perhaps interspersed with music. If the latter idea appeals to you but your group is not a particularly musical one, then consider working together with a local Christian band or singing group who complement your style or appeal to the particular age group at which you are aiming.

If the performance is to be longer than an hour, then it is best to plan a short interval at half-time. If you have someone to organize refreshments they could be served at this point, or saved until the end of the performance when they will encourage the audience to stay and chat to each other and to the actors about what the evening has conveyed.

Some practical points

People usually most appreciate the value of something if they have to pay for it. You may find that you will attract far more people to a performance by making a small charge and selling tickets beforehand.

Publicity, of course, is a very important aspect of the organization of a special event. It should not be treated lightly, but be taken on by someone who has an interest and a flair for it. If you are trying to attract non-Christians, then you will need to take particular care over publicity. Any title which you decide upon must be intriguing, whilst not giving away all the secrets of your performance. Try to think of a title which is short, to the point and will stick in people's minds.

Posters should be kept as simple and uncluttered as possible giving only the vital details about time, place, date etc. If your group performs regularly in an area, it can be helpful for you to adopt a visual symbol or particular type of lettering which people will recognize at a glance. Depending on the age and type of audience you want to attract you may find it useful to publicize your event through local community centres, schools, and youth clubs, as well as the normal church channels and local shop windows.

Entertainment

You would never think to try and convert a starving beggar without also offering him food; remember that in the same way your audiences are hungry for entertainment. You must fulfil that need through your drama, always entertaining in order to earn the right to share your message with them.

> "To them you are nothing more than an entertainer singing love songs or playing a harp. They listen to all your words and don't obey a single one of them. But when all your words come true . . . then they will know that a prophet has been among them."
>
> *Ezekiel 33. 32-33*

4 Sample Scripts

The Two Builders

(The parable of the wise and foolish man)

This is a very simple, but lively way of presenting the parable in Matthew 7.24-27. It uses the words of Jesus from the Good News Bible and illustrates them rather literally, the actors providing a kind of moving visual aid. The two main characters here are "stock" types. P. P. Browne a bespectacled intellectual, Gumby the Monty Python type "twit". The Assistant plays the role of a frantic stage manager and "effects" person. Each time his or her services are required, he runs forward, provides the necessary sound or visual effect and then runs back to the props table to await the next instruction.

Characters:
Narrator, Assistant, 4 people who make "House", P. P. Browne, Gumby.

[Downstage right is an empty chair. There is a table with props upstage left. Upstage centre with backs to audience in the order (stage right to left) are: Narrator, "House", Assistant, who form a line. P. P. Browne, and Gumby, are hidden in front of them, i.e. further upstage. At a given signal Narrator rushes downstage right and on to chair. Assistant rushes downstage left]

Assistant:	*[as if trumpet fanfare]* Da-daah!
Narrator:	Jesus said, Anyone who hears my words, and obeys them, is like . . . a wise man.
	[P. P. Browne emerges from behind "house" line and comes to stand downstage left]
Assistant:	*[as before]* Da-daah!
P. P. Browne:	Good evening. P. P. Browne's the name, Brown with an "e". *[pause]* B.A. Honours. First actually, from Cambridge, in Architecture.
Narrator:	Who built his house on rock.
P. P. Browne:	*[searching ground for rock]* Erm, let me see. Ah, yes; here we are. *[Assistant picks up tambour or drum and bangs it three times as P. P. Browne mimes banging his foot on rock.]* Good solid ground this, what? *[claps twice]*
	[the 4 people walk downstage and stand two on either side of P. P. Browne facing each other. They raise their arms to form a roof over his head]
Narrator:	The wind blew hard. *[Assistant runs forward and blows very gently at group, then returns to position at props table]* The wind blew *hard*! *[Assistant blows with all his might]* The rivers . . . *[Assistant picks up a cup of water, takes a mouthful, and gargles loudly]* . . . overflowed. *[Assistant spurts mouthful of water over house]* The rain . . . *[Assistant picks up full watering can and shows it to audience]* . . . poured down. *[Assistant pours water all over house]* But, that house did not fall. Because it was built on rock. *[Assistant picks up tambour or drum and bangs it three times as P. P. Browne mimes as before]*
P. P. Browne:	Good solid ground this, what?
Narrator:	But. Anyone who hears my words and does not obey them, is like a foolish man.

	[*Gumby turns and walks downstage right. He stands level with **P. P.** Browne*]
Assistant:	[*as before*] Da-daah!
Gumby:	Hullo. A. Gumby, builder's mate.
Narrator:	Who built . . . his house . . . on sand.
	[*Assistant brings Gumby a bucket and spade. Gumby then scoops up two shovelsful of sand and puts them in the bucket*]
Gumby:	Pretty sand. [*he puts down bucket and spade, and lines up his hands to clap as **P. P. Browne** has done. His two attempts result in his hands failing to make contact*]
	[*Assistant runs on and claps for him, picks up bucket and spade and returns to position. On hearing the clap, the **House** moves across stage and adopts the same position around **Gumby***]
Narrator:	The wind blew hard. [*Assistant comes forward and blows at the house with all his might. **House** drops by bending knees, making creaking noises*] The rivers . . . [*Assistant as before*] . . . overflowed. [*Gumby stands slowly; **Assistant** takes another mouthful of water, unseen by **Gumby**, and spurts it in **Gumby's** face*] The rain . . . [*Assistant as before*] . . . poured down. [*Assistant pours water over **Gumby***] And that house fell. [*House falls to crouching position, creaking*] And what a terrible fall that was! [*Assistant bangs tambour or drum several times, **House** all roll backwards, and lie with their arms and legs in the air. **Assistant** replaces tambour or drum, and comes downstage centre*]
Assistant:	[*to audience*] And so you can see from our story that all people are fools!
Narrator:	Hey! There was a wise person in that story.
	[*Assistant looks puzzled. He turns to **Gumby**, then looks back to audience still more puzzled. He turns to **P. P. Browne** and gasps*]
Assistant:	So there was! [*runs to fallen **House** to share good news*] We've found a wise man . . . a wise man . . . we've found a wise man!!
House:	[*getting to their feet*] Where?
Assistant:	[*pointing to **P. P. Browne***] There!
	[*House gasps. **Narrator**, **Assistant**, **Gumby**, and **House** come out of character, run across to a surprised **P. P. Browne**, and become T.V. reporters crouched on the floor around him holding imaginary microphones. The following questions numbered 1 to 7 are divided up amongst the cast*]
All:	[*except **P. P. Browne**, in unison*] Question, question, question, question, question.

P. P. Browne:	Which one shall I answer first?
All:	*[as before]* Question, question, question, question, question.
1:	Why didn't your house fall down?
P. P. Browne:	Because I built it on rock.
2:	That's because you've got a degree in architecture.
P. P. Browne:	No.
3:	Is it because you went to Cambridge University?
P. P. Browne:	No.
4:	Is it because you're incredibly clever?
P. P. Browne:	*[becoming more emphatic]* No!
5:	Is it because you're posh?
P. P. Browne:	No!
All:	*[except **P. P. Browne**, in unison]* Why is it then?
P. P. Browne:	*[drops character — by taking off glasses — and becomes "straight"]* Well look. This story . . . it's a parable, and . . .
6:	*[interrupting]* What's a parable?
P. P. Browne:	A parable? Well, it's a story that's got another meaning . . . and in this . . .
7:	*[interrupting]* What does it mean?
P. P. Browne:	*[not nastily]* I'm trying to tell you. *[pause]* The rock is like Jesus; and I'm building my life on Him!
All:	*[as before, not really seeing at all]* Oh!
P. P. Browne:	Now do you see?
All:	*[realizing]* Jesus!
P. P. Browne:	*[encouraging]* Yes!
All:	*[as before, turning to audience and speaking into their microphones]* What a wise man! *[freeze]*

The Story of Little Billy and Big Joe

(The parable of the rich fool)

This has proved to be one of our most popular sketches, and although the script may appear complex, the story itself is a simple one (it is based on Luke 12.13-21) and is easily followed by people of all ages. — Quite apart from that it is great fun to do! Any similarity between the singing of the girls and the fifties' style record "Leader of the Pack" by the Shangri-Las is not at all accidental — try and dig up a copy.

Characters:

Narrator, an American baseball coach type loudmouth. Little Billy, a downtrodden American kid. Big Joe, a Mr. Universe type bully-biker and 2 Girls of the American fifties' teenage variety (chewing gum etc.)

[Narrator stands in a raised position (a chair will do) downstage left. Big Joe stands near to him, on his right, back to the audience. The two Girls stand lined up in front of Big Joe (upstage) also with backs to audience. Little Billy is standing stage right facing the audience]

Narrator: Friends! I wanna tell y'all a story about motorsickles! It takes place in Townsville, Arizona. And over here we have Little Billy! *[he indicates Billy who looks up at audience, grins, and during the following speech he walks backwards and forwards across the stage]* Every morning Little Billy goes shopping with his Ma and his Pa, and there is nothing — not one thing, friends — that little Billy likes more than looking in motorsickle shops!

Billy: *[looking in imaginary shop window]* Oh wow! Look at the boikes in this motorsickle shop! Gee, Dad! When can I get a boike like that? I gotta get one so that I can be like my hero Big Joe!

Narrator: Big Joe is the coolest . . . the slickest biker in the whole of Arizona. Big Joe is rough! *[Joe and the Girls turn to face audience, still in single file]* Big Joe is tough! *[they mime sitting on a large motorbike]* And Big Joe's gotta B.M.W. RS 900! *[2 Girls look over Joe's shoulders]*

Girls: *[singing]* That's why we fell for the leader of the pack!

Joe: *[revving up his bike]* Brrrmm! Brrrmm! Shucks, folks! *[he grins at audience. Billy looks at him in admiration and awe]*

Narrator: One day, Little Billy gets the chance of a lifetime when he's offered a job in a motorsickle repair shop!

Billy: Ow wow! A job in a motorsickle repair shop. Now I can work with the boikes that I've always loved! *[he comes downstage centre and works on an imaginary motorbike]*

Narrator: And friends, Little Billy's bliss turns to pure ecstacy when, who should come into the shop but his hero, Big Joe!

Joe: Brrrmm! *[he rides into workshop, Girls riding pillion. They screech to a halt stage right of Billy and climb off the bike]*

Billy: *[admiringly]* Hi there, Big Joe!

Joe: Hi there, Little Billy. Hey son! Set the tappets on my machine.

Billy: Sure thing, Big Joe! *[he works on Joe's bike with imaginary spanners etc.]*

Joe: And make it snappy. *[he looks at Girls]* I got work to attend to!

Girls: Oooh!

Billy: O.K. Big Joe.

Joe: And don't get your greasy digits on my crankcase, boy.

Billy: I'll try not to, Big Joe. They should be O.K. now, Big Joe. *[he gets up]* Mind if I have a sit on your boike? *[he jumps on]*

Girls: Aaah! Ain't he sweet?

Joe: Get off my bike, small fry! *[pushes him off the bike]*

Billy: Sorry, Big Joe.
[the Girls are standing either side of Big Joe looking at him adoringly]

Girl A: Ain't he rough?

Girl B: Ain't he tough?

Both: An' ain't he got a B.M.W. RS 900? *[singing]* That's why we fell for the leader of the pack!

Joe: Brrrmm! Brrrmm! Shucks, folks! See ya, Billy! *[they jump on the bike and roar back to their position stage left. Billy looks after them]*

Narrator: Little Billy is determined to get a motorsickle!

Billy: Aw gee! I just gotta get me a motorsickle! I ain't never gonna get anywhere in life until I get me a boike like Big Joe's. I'm gonna work real hard, and save me up some money.

Narrator: And so, he works hard.

Billy: *[going through a set of simple, repetitive movements which suggest working hard, and chanting]* Honda! Kawasaki! Suzuki! Yamaha!

Narrator: And he works harder!

Billy: *[moving and chanting faster]* Honda! Kawasaki! Suzuki! Yamaha!

Narrator: And he works harder!

Billy: *[faster]* Honda! Kawasaki! Suzuki! Yamaha!

Narrator: Until one day . . . *[Billy looks at him in anticipation]* he can afford his very

	first motorsickle. *[he throws **Billy** a helmet]*
Billy:	Wow! My very first boike! *[puts on helmet and mimes climbing onto a ridiculously small bike]*

Billy: Wow! My very first boike! *[puts on helmet and mimes climbing onto a ridiculously small bike]*

Narrator: Little Billy is rough! Little Billy is tough! And Little Billy's got a fifty c.c. moped!

Girls: *[running forward to stand on either side of him, sing]* That's why we call him the leader of the pack! *[**Billy** revs up his bike but instead of producing a great roar it makes a sound like a couple of feeble "raspberries"]*

Girl A: Hi, Billy!

Girl B: Hi, Billy!

Billy: Hi there, girls!

Girl A: Hey, Billy, you gotta bike!

Girl B: And what a bike! *[they both laugh]*

Billy: Yeah! *[indignantly]* Why don't you jump on the back of it, and I'll take you for a ride!

Girls: *[climbing on]* Ooh! *[as they sit down they make noises expressing distaste at the size of the bike]*

Billy: Hold tight now, girls. *[he revs the engine again, but it splutters to a halt]*

Joe: Brrrmm! *[he drives up, screeching to a halt beside **Billy**]* Hi there, Billy! *[laughs]* Say, what are you doing sitting on that toy, boy? Hop on, girls, let's go for a real ride. *[the **Girls** climb off **Billy's** bike and onto **Joe's**]* See ya, Billy!

Girls: See ya, Billy, bye, Billy *[etc.]*
*[they drive off back to their position stage left, **Billy** climbs off his bike]*

Narrator: Little Billy is crestfallen.

Billy: Oh gee, I'm crestfallen. I ain't never gonna get anywhere with a stupid little moped. I gotta get me a real sickle! I'm gonna work real hard, sell everything I own and save up all my money until I can buy the biggest sickle in the whole of Arizona!

Narrator: And so he works even harder than before.

Billy: *[resuming the actions and the rhythmic chant even faster than before, and sustaining it throughout the **Narrator's** speech]* Honda! Kawasaki! Suzuki! Yamaha!

Narrator: He works overtime . . . he works his weekends . . . the bank holidays, and all the days in between. And he works harder, and he rides harder, and he saves harder and he fills up his piggy bank and then . . . *[**Billy** stops and looks at **Narrator** hopefully]* . . . he buys a bigger piggy bank and works three times as hard!

Billy: *[looking daggers at **Narrator** then resuming chant, louder and almost furiously]* Honda! Kawasaki! Suzuki! Yamaha!

Narrator: *[butting in and stopping **Billy**]* And then . . . his bikes begin to get bigger. *[**Billy** jumps onto a medium sized bike]* And bigger! *[**Billy** as before, only the bike is obviously larger]* and BIGGER! *[this time the bike is colossal]* Until he has the biggest cotton pickin' bike in the whole of Arizona! *[**Billy** sits proudly on his bike downstage centre]*

Joe: Brrrmm! *[drives up, with **Girls**, beside **Billy**]*

Narrator: Big Joe is rough! Big Joe is tough! And Big Joe's got a B.M.W. RS 900!

Girls: *[sing]* That's why we fell for the leader of the pack!

Joe: Brrrmm! Brrrmm! Shucks, folks!

Billy: *[revving up his enormously powerful engine]* Veroom! Veroom!

Girls: Oooh! *[they climb off Joe's bike and go over to **Billy**, standing one either side of him as with **Joe** earlier]*

Girl A: Billy is rougher!

Girl B: Billy is tougher!

Both: And Billy's got a Harley Davidson twelve hundred! *[sing]* That's why we fell for the leader of the pack!

Billy: *[revs his engine again]* Veroom! Veroom!

Joe: *[with pathos]* Shucks, folks . . . *[he returns crestfallen to his position stage left]*

Billy: D'ya wanna go for a proper ride?

Girls: Oooh!

Billy: Jump on the back then! *[they climb onto the enormous bike with difficulty, squealing with excitement]* O.K. hold tight now y'all! Veroom! *[they circle around the stage and screech to a halt upstage left, near **Big Joe**, where the **Girls** jump off the bike]*

Girl A: Thanks, Billy!

Girl B: It was great, Billy!

Billy: See ya in the morning, girls!

Girls: Bye, Billy! Bye!

Billy: Bye! *[he rides back to downstage centre, where he stays, facing the audience, riding his bike]* This is the life! Boiking down the freeway at 95. Now I got everything I need, everything I saved up for. I got the boike, I got the girls, I got everything I need in the world. *[reacting suddenly]* What's that jerk doing on the wrong side of the road! *[he swerves from side to side]*

Narrator, Joe, Girls: *[in unison]* Look out, Billy!

*[**Girls** scream loudly. **Billy** is thrown from his bike, landing heavily on*

the ground, he rolls around before dying. **Big Joe** comes forward to stand by **Billy's** body, helmet to chest, head bowed. Whilst the **Narrator** delivers the closing speech the **Girls** provide a continuous, mournful, but tuneful musical backing]

Girls: [singing] Oooh, ooh, ooh!

Narrator: [standing over **Billy's** body, cap in hand] And, dear friends, it says in the Bible: Watch out and guard yourselves from every kind of greed, because a person's true life is not made up of the things he owns, no matter how rich he may be. Amen.

[he bows his head. Big Joe grins at audience]

A Tale of Two Men

(The parable of the Pharisee and the tax collector)
The chorus in this sketch (which is based on Luke 18.9-14) acts as narrator, sometimes acting and speaking as one man, sometimes in sequence. Actions should usually accompany their speeches. These have sometimes been suggested in the script, but otherwise a group should invent their own. The important thing is that whether the chorus mime an action together, or individually, it should be co-ordinated to the rhythm of the speech.

Characters:
Mr. Arnold church caretaker with a strong northern accent, Chorus of two people (individually referred to as A and B), Arthur Bigshot, Slimy Eric.

[Chorus in formation with back to audience, and with hands in praying position. Enter Mr. Arnold pushing a broom and whistling to himself, stops downstage centre, in front of Chorus]

Mr. Arnold:	Oh, hello. St. Stephen's church. Me? Mr. Arnold, church caretaker. Vicar says I've got to sweep up before that lot comes in. I says 'It's a waste of time, they'll only make a mess again' . . . but vicar knows best. Hey up! *[enter chorus]* Here they come, better make myself scarce. *[retires stage right]*
Chorus:	*[enter and stand side by side, downstage centre, with a space in between for central characters to enter. As each starts to speak, they lower their hands to their sides]*
A:	There were once two men.
B:	Who went to church.
A:	To pray to God.
B:	One was a good and well-respected man. *[both indicate A. Bigshot as he enters]*
Bigshot:	*[proudly]* You all know me.
Chorus:	We all know him.
Bigshot:	A good man.
Chorus:	A fine man.
Bigshot:	Today I shall pray to God.
A:	He's gonna pray!
B:	He's gonna pray!

Chorus: He's gonna pray! *[a clap can indicate the end of this sequence]*
[the next sequence can be mimed literally]

A: And so he went.

B: On his way to church, giving money to the poor.

Chorus: And the sick.

A: And he reached the church.

B: And went inside.

A: Took off his hat.

B: And prayed.

Bigshot: *[confidently to the heavens]* You know me, God.

A: *[admiringly]* A good man.

B: *[admiringly]* A fine man.

Bigshot: I've grafted hard.

A: An honest,

B: Hard-working,

Chorus: Man.

Bigshot: I've given money to nine different charities.

A: A generous,

B: Big-hearted,

Chorus: Man.

Bigshot: I give ten percent of everything to the church.

A: A devout,

B: Religious,

Chorus: Man.

Bigshot: I say my prayers every morning.

Chorus: Surely this man is a saint! *[they make a halo around **Bigshot's** head with their hands. As they do they say . . .]*
PING!

Bigshot: So I thank thee, God, that I'm not like other men — *[**Chorus** break, and resume original "praying" position, with heads bowed]* the swindlers, the cheats, the spongers, the thieves, the muggers, the murderers, the winos, the tramps, and the no-good filthy sinners of this town! And especially that I'm not like Slimy Eric!
*[during this speech, **Bigshot** steps out to stage left to make room for **Slimy Eric**, who now enters between **Chorus** making apt noises — i.e. throat clearing and coughing]*
*[**Chorus**, scornfully]*

A: The other was a common criminal.

B: A no-good thief.

A:	A dirty layabout.
B:	Name of . . .
Chorus:	Slimy Eric!
Slimy Eric:	*[cringing in anticipation]* You all know me.
Chorus:	*[cynically]* We all know him.
Slimy Eric:	Not a good man.
Chorus:	A rotten stinking sinner!
Slimy Eric:	But I will try and pray to God.
A:	He's gonna pray.
B:	He's gonna pray.
Chorus:	He's gonna pray. *[this sequence can be said with an air of disbelief and with a "huh!" instead of a clap]*
A:	And so he came.
B:	Up to church.
A:	For the very first time.
B:	In a stolen car.
A:	And he reached the church.
B:	And went inside.
A:	And bowed his head.
B:	And prayed.
Chorus:	Dirty sinner!
Slimy Eric:	You know me, God. *[said tentatively]*
A:	A bad man.
B:	An evil man.
Slimy Eric:	I've wasted my time.
A:	An idler.
B:	A layabout.
Slimy Eric:	I've pinched handbags, stolen cars.
A:	A pickpocket.
B:	A car thief.
Slimy Eric:	I've even taken lollipops off little kids.
A:	A coward.
B:	A . . .
Chorus:	Slimy Eric!
Slimy Eric:	And I've never prayed in my life.
Chorus:	*[accusingly]* God will never listen to him! *[they point their fingers over **Slimy Eric's** head, forcing him to cringe even lower]*
Slimy Eric:	*[miserably]* Oh God, what can I say? *[moves out to stage right]* I'm no good . . . I've never worked . . . I've never been near a charity in my life.

And if I'd have gone to church, I'd probably have nicked the collection plate. But I want to change my wicked ways. I'm not a good man . . . I'm just sorry!

A: So the two men prayed.

B: And waited to see.

A: Which of their prayers.

B: God would accept.

Chorus: One.

A: A good man.

B: A fine man.

Bigshot: You know me, God.

Chorus: The other.

B: A bad man.

A: An evil man.

Slimy Eric: I'm sorry.

Chorus: One, a hard-working man.

Bigshot: Graft! Grafted hard!

Chorus: The other, an idle layabout.

Slimy Eric: *[with added pathos each time]* I'm sorry.

Chorus: One, a generous man.

Bigshot: Nine different charities, mind.

Chorus: The other, a no-good thief.

Slimy Eric: I'm sorry.

Chorus: One, a religious man.

Bigshot: Pray every morning.

Chorus: The other, a slimy Eric!

Slimy Eric: *[almost inaudible now]* I'm sorry.

Chorus: Which prayer will God accept? Surely the prayer of . . .

A: A devout man *[each member of Chorus move to Bigshot as they speak]*

B: A religious man.

A: A righteous man.

B: A godly man.

Chorus: A faithful, great and saintly man! *[during last speech, Chorus lift Bigshot into the air]*

[Mr. Arnold, who has been observing the scene from stage right, now comes in between Slimy Eric and Chorus]

Mr. Arnold: 'Ere, just a minute.

Chorus:	Ssshhh!
Mr. Arnold:	You've got it wrong.
Chorus:	Ssshhh!
Mr. Arnold:	No, but it says in the Bible. *[indicates his pocket New Testament]*
Chorus:	*[cutting him short]* Sssshhhh!
Mr. Arnold:	It says in the Bible that God listened to *him*. *[indicates Slimy Eric]*
Chorus:	What?
Mr. Arnold:	Aye, he *[indicates Bigshot]* made out he were perfect, but he *[indicates Slimy Eric]* knew he were wrong, and were sorry.
Chorus:	Whaat?
Mr. Arnold:	So God listened to him!
Chorus:	*[dropping Bigshot]* Whaaat?!
Bigshot:	Oww!
Slimy Eric:	*[looking up]* Thank you, God. *[during the following sequence Slimy Eric moves slowly backwards to upstage right, "appealing" to Chorus. They move, each on their speech to upstage centre — keeping to the original formation. They are aghast]*
Chorus:	Slimy Eric?
B:	Slimy Eric?
A:	Slimy Eric?
Chorus:	Slimy Eric? Huh! *[they turn their backs sharply, returning to original positions. Slimy Eric turns also]*
Mr. Arnold:	*[returning to his work]* Some people never learn.
Bigshot:	I'll make it thirty-two different charities. *[plaintively looking up to God, and anyone else who will listen]*
Mr. Arnold:	Come on, off you go. I've got to get this place cleared up. *[advances towards Bigshot with broom]*
Bigshot:	All right, I'll pray twice a day!
Mr. Arnold:	Look, you're in me way. Go on, off home.
Bigshot:	O.K. three times. I'll pray three times every morning!
Mr. Arnold:	I've got to clear up. Just be off out of it. *[now pushing Bigshot with his broom]*
Bigshot:	*[desperately]* I'll pray four times, I can't say fairer!
Mr. Arnold:	*[quite annoyed by now]* I've got be home for me tea by five!
Bigshot:	Five! I'll pray five times a day!
Mr. Arnold:	*[shoves him off]* Go on. Out you go!
Bigshot:	*[collects himself, and starts to walk off (upstage) with as much dignity as possible, then turns back for one last try]* O.K. I'll come to —

Mr. Arnold: *[shouts] Goodnight!*
*[**Bigshot** turns his back as before, and freezes]*
I said it were a waste of time. *[freeze]*

Special Offer

(The parable of the sower)

This sketch has proved effective in almost every type of performance — it works well when done flamboyantly for street theatre, but is not out of place in a family service or school assembly, particularly at Harvest Festival time as it is based on the parable of the sower. The dialogue uses many rhythmic patterns and it is important that these should be developed, not only in Reginald Melling's speeches, but also in his exchanges with the other characters.

Characters:

Reginald Melling a door-to-door salesman, **Posh Lady**, **Hippie**, **Worried Man**, **Young Man**.

[All except Reginald Melling stand upstage in a line, in above order (stage left to right) with backs to audience. They freeze. Reginald Melling is downstage centre, back to audience. He is carrying a bag which contains three bananas. He turns round and addresses audience]

Reginald Melling:	How do you do! Hello, how are you!
	I'm Reginald Melling, and I go out selling.
	But today, special day! Giving samples away.
	No conning, you'll see, special offer: it's free!
	Ladies and Gentlemen, I have in this bag, a brand new product. Never seen, tasted, smelt or felt before. Without more ado, I unveil to you . . . *[dips hand in bag and pulls out]* . . . a *banana*! Yes, it really is a banana. Ordinary people *[indicates other four]* in this ordinary street, have never, never tasted the delights of the banana before.
	[goes up to Posh Lady (stage left) mimes knocking at the door in time with the words]
	Knock! Knock! Knock! Knock! *[she turns round and looks at him questioningly]* How do you do?
Posh Lady:	Hello, who are you?
Reginald Melling:	I'm Reginald Melling.
Posh Lady:	Oh, what are you selling?
Reginald Melling:	Not selling, it's free!
Posh Lady:	*[excited]* Well, what can it be?
Reginald Melling:	It is called *[producing a banana]* . . . a *banana*!

Posh Lady:	Oh. *[distastefully]* How nice. How twee. You're saying it's free?
Reginald Melling:	You eat it.
Posh Lady:	Oh well . . . perhaps I'll try it sometime. Thank you for calling. Good morning! *[throws banana up in the air.* **Reginald Melling** *catches it in his bag. She turns around and freezes again]*
Reginald Melling:	*[shrugs shoulders and takes two steps to next person in time to words]* Oh, well, can't win them all. *[mimes as before]* Knock! Knock! Knock! Knock! *[Hippie turns to look at him]* How do you do?
Hippie:	*[Vaguely]* Hi! Who are you?
Reginald Melling:	I'm Reginald Melling.
Hippie:	*[cynically]* Oh, what are you selling?
Reginald Melling:	Not selling, it's free!
Hippie:	*[more interested]* Wow! What can it be?
Reginald Melling:	It's called *[producing a banana]* . . . a *banana*!
Hippie:	Hey man, that's really free! Really yellow! Really bent! *[holding up banana and becoming progressively more excited]* It looks cosmic . . . It smells cosmic . . . It feels cosmic!
Reginald Melling:	You eat it.
Hippie:	Far out! *[bites banana with skin on]* Yeuk! *[drops banana,* **Reginald Melling** *catches it]* That is uncool! *[turns and freezes again]*
Reginald Melling:	*[moving as before]* Oh well . . . can't win them all. *[as before]* Knock! Knock! Knock! Knock! *[Worried Man turns to look at him]* How do you do?
Worried Man:	*[looking harrassed]* Hello . . . who are you?
Reginald Melling:	I'm Reginald Melling.
Worried Man:	Oh, what are you selling?
Reginald Melling:	Not selling, it's free.
Worried Man:	Well, what can it be?
Reginald Melling:	It's called *[producing a banana]* . . . a *banana*!
Worried Man:	Will it take my mind off all my worries?
Reginald Melling:	It might do, you eat it.
Worried Man:	I haven't got much time for eating, but I'll give it a try. *[starts to peel banana]* *[the other three characters remain with their backs to the audience and assume "different" voices. They shout]*
Hippie:	Dad!
Posh Lady:	Darling!
Young Man:	'Ere mate!

Worried Man:	*[looking around nervously]* See what I mean, so many calls on my time! *[peels a bit more]*
Hippie:	Dad! Will you give us a hand with the car?
Posh Lady:	Darling, you haven't paid that electricity bill!
Young Man:	'Ere mate, you owe me some money!
Worried Man:	Oh! It will have to be a quick one! *[puts banana to mouth]* *[the three voices shout together, improvising various demands for approximately five seconds, stopping as **Worried Man** exclaims]*
Worried Man:	Oooh! I've only got one pair of hands! *[squeezes banana, crushing it]* Eeurgh! *[turns and freezes again]*
Reginald Melling:	*[moving as before]* Oh well . . . can't win them all. *[as before]* Knock! Knock! Knock! Knock! *[**Young Man** turns to look at him]* How do you do?
Young Man:	*[bright and interested]* Hello, who are you?
Reginald Melling:	I'm Reginald Melling.
Young Man:	Oh, what are you selling?
Reginald Melling:	Not selling, it's free.
Young Man:	Well, what can it be?
Reginald Melling:	It's called *[as before]* . . . a *banana*!
Young Man:	Oh great! *[taking banana and putting it to his ear like a telephone]* Hello Mum? *[laughs]* What do you do with it?
Reginald Melling:	You eat it.
Young Man:	Oh, you *eat* it. *[tries to fit it in his mouth]* How?
Reginald Melling:	You peel it.
Young Man:	Oh I see . . . like this. *[peels slowly]* How novel! What will they think of next? *[eats. A smile gradually spreading over his face]* Mmmmm! It's great! Fantastic! Taste and see how good it is! *[runs into the audience offering bites of the banana to three or four people, and improvising comments. Runs back into position]* Fantastic! *[turns and freezes again]*
Reginald Melling:	*[to audience]* Giving away bananas is just like trying to tell people about Jesus. Some people say . . . *[indicates **Posh Lady**]*
Posh Lady:	*[turning around]* Not today thank you, I'm not interested. *[freezes in position]*
Reginald Melling:	Other people say . . . *[indicates **Hippie**]*
Hippie:	*[turning around]* Tried it once, couldn't keep it up . . . too much like hard work. *[freezes in position]*
Reginald Melling:	Others say . . . *[indicates **Worried Man**]*

Worried Man:	*[turning around]* I'd love to, but I've got so much on my mind. *[freezes in position]*
Reginald Melling:	But some people say . . . *[indicating **Young Man**]*
Young Man:	*[turning around]* It's great! Fantastic! Taste and see how good he is! *[freezes in position]*
Reginald Melling:	*[still to audience]* We offer Jesus Christ to you!
All:	Taste and see what he can do!

The last line can be accompanied by group movement. Suggestions:

Taste	*All look stage right and point to mouth.*
and see	*All look stage left and shield eyes.*
what he	*All lift arms and look up.*
can do	*All spread arms to front, the back line standing upright, Reginald Melling with knees bent. Hold for count of three.*

The Race

A very simple allegory which represents life as a race (see Philippians 3.14), and tries to show the different things that people think will get them into heaven. A lively pace should be maintained throughout the piece, becoming more frantic as it reaches its conclusion — aim to make the audience feel as exhausted as the actors themselves.

Characters:
Commentator, **Miss Hegginbottom** an affluent lady, **Rev. MacWhirter** a vicar, **P. C. Plod** a policeman.

*[The three runners stand in a diagonal line stage right, facing a finishing tape which is held opposite to them stage left. They warm up for the race, whilst **Commentator** standing downstage centre introduces the scene]*

Commentator:	*[bright and animated]* Ladies and Gentlemen, welcome on this bright and sunny afternoon to the race course of life. Here this afternoon, on this very race course, we're running a very special race with the once in a lifetime chance for our three contestants to get themselves into heaven. Yes, they have a limited amount of time this afternoon, to get themselves into heaven. Let me introduce you to our three runners. In the far lane we have Miss Hegginbottom...*[**Miss Hegginbottom** trots downstage centre and vainly acknowledges the audience]*
Miss Hegginbottom:	Hello! *[returns to her position in line]*
Commentator:	A pretty young filly, who's in very good shape indeed and stands a good chance of winning the race, and getting into heaven this afternoon. In

the centre lane we have the Reverend MacWhirter . . . *[Rev. MacWhirter runs downstage centre and nods to audience]*

Rev. MacWhirter: Jumble sale Saturday two o'clock *[returns to position]*

Commentator: A local vicar who's been practising what he preaches all week, and also stands a very good chance of getting into heaven this afternoon. And in the nearside lane, we have P.C. Plod . . . *[P.C. Plod plods downstage centre]*

P.C. Plod: Evening all! *[returns to position in line]*

Commentator: A local policeman who thinks he's going to win the race because of the size of his feet. And they're all warming up now for the start . . . they're under starter's orders . . . and . . . *[hooter sounds]* . . . They're off! *[all three characters start running on the spot, this is maintained thoughout the sketch. The Commentator has taken up a raised position upstage)* And here they come steaming up the track. And yes, I think Miss Hegginbottom's going to say something first . . .

Miss Hegginbottom: I'm a very nice person! *[trots forward a few feet towards the tape]*

Commentator: She's a very nice person and that takes her into the lead, ahead of all the others, nearer to heaven than the rest of them. Rev. MacWhirter it's your turn now . . .

Rev. MacWhirter: I'm a vicar! *[runs forward overtaking Miss Hegginbottom by a few feet]*

Commentator: Yes, he's a vicar! And that takes him into the lead ahead of Miss Hegginbottom. What a turn up for the books, it must be better to be a vicar than to be a nice person. And yes, yes, it's over to P.C. Plod . . .

P.C. Plod: I'm a policeman! *[runs heavily on the spot hardly moving forward at all]*

Commentator: He is indeed a policeman, but that doesn't get him very far. Never mind, P.C. Plod *[Miss Hegginbottom's feather boa slips from her shoulders to the ground]* Oh dear! Miss Hegginbottom seems to have lost part of her clothing. Will she stop to pick up her feather boa, or will she go ahead into the lead?

Miss Hegginbottom: *[looking back towards her boa, hesitating but then deciding to go on with the race]* I can help with meals on wheels! *[she overtakes vicar. The pace is becoming frantic]*

Commentator: She helps with meals on wheels and she's left it behind and gone ahead into the lead, nearer to heaven than the rest of them. Come on vicar you can't let her win!

Rev. MacWhirter: I can preach for three hours without a drink of water! *[he overtakes Miss Hegginbottom]*

Commentator: *[getting more and more excited]* He can preach for three hours without

	a drink of water! Yes, he's gone into the lead. He's in the very forefront of the race. This is very exciting! Come on, it's your chance to catch up now, P.C. Plod!
P.C. Plod:	I've never done anything wrong! *[moves ahead slightly]*
Commentator:	He says he's never done anything wrong . . . but that doesn't get him very far either. Never mind, P.C. Plod. Yes, oh, wait a minute . . . Miss Hegginbottom is looking back towards her clothing. Do her possessions mean more to her than getting into heaven? *[Miss Hegginbottom hesitates, torn between her feather boa and reaching heaven. She decides on the boa and runs back to pick it up]* Yes, she's gone back to pick up her feather boa and lost her chance. She's out of the race and it looks certain that the vicar is going to win!
Rev. MacWhirter:	I've read the Bible from cover to cover! *[moves into the lead a few feet from the tape]*
Commentator:	He's read the Bible from cover to cover and he's nearly there, he's nearly in heaven but not quite. Come on, P.C. Plod, this is your last chance!
P.C. Plod:	I believe in God! *[moves forward a few paces]*
Commentator:	He believes in God!
P.C. Plod:	I believe in the Devil *[moves forward a few more]*
Commentator:	He believes in the Devil!
P.C. Plod:	And I believe in the Bible! *[overtakes the vicar, very nearly reaching the finishing tape]*
Commentator:	He believes in the Bible! And he's nearly there and it looks . . . *[the hooter interrupts, signalling the end of time. The runners freeze in their positions. Commentator speaks more slowly and quietly — moving downstage centre]* Ladies and Gentlemen. Time is up. None of these good people, no matter how hard they tried, could get themselves into heaven this afternoon . . . For they all lacked the one vital ingredient in their lives it takes to get you there.
	[all hold freeze]

©Footprints Theatre Company 1979

Bibliography

Resources from the Bible Society

The Bible Society has many resources to help you to use the Bible in drama. As well as the products already mentioned in this book, we can supply you with:
Bibles, New Testaments, Portions and many other things.
   Write for a catalogue containing details of all our materials to:
The Development Consultant
Bible Society
146 Queen Victoria Street
London EC4V 4BX

To help you in designing sessions

Children's Games of Street and Playground by Peter and Iona Opie: Oxford University Press
I'm Four Potatoes: Drama for Schools by Dawn Anderson: Primary Education Publishing Ltd
Theatre Games by Clive Barker: Eyre Methuen
Improvisation by John Hodgson and Ernest Richards: Eyre Methuen
Voice and Speech in the Theatre by James C. Turner: Pitman
Anthology of British Tongue Twisters by Ken Parkin: Samuel French

To help with Bible study

The Lion Handbook to the Bible: Lion Publishing
Jesus and the Four Gospels by John Drane: Lion Publishing

Scripts

Time to Act by Paul Burbridge and Murray Watts: Hodder & Stoughton
The Playbook: For Christian Theater: Young Calvanists Federation, Box 7244, Grand Rapids, Michigan, MI 49510
What Next by Peter Cotterell: Lakeland